Design&Knit
the Sweater of Your Dreams

J. Marsha Michler

Published by

**krause
publications**

700 East State Street • Iola, WI 54990-0001
715/445-2214 • FAX: 715/445-4087   www.krause.com

Please call or write for our free catalog of publications. To place
an order or obtain a free catalog, please call (800) 258-0929, or
please use our regular business telephone:
(715) 445-2214.

Library of Congress Catalog Number: 2001099543
ISBN: 0-87349-329-X

Every effort has been made to produce the highest degree of accuracy of
the contents of this book. Author or publisher is not responsible for any
human or typographical errors that may have occurred. Graphs, diagrams,
and instructions may be photocopied for personal use only. Designs are not to
be knitted for any commercial purposes.

DESIGN AND KNIT THE SWEATER OF YOUR DREAMS

DEDICATION

To mom the artist, pianist, seamstress, knitter, designer of houses and gardens, raiser of five kids, spinner, dyer, weaver who had the foresight to give me the tools at an early age and to allow the creative use of them is, ever was, and always will be my inspiration and role model.

ACKNOWLEDGMENTS

A great many thanks to my agent, Sandy Taylor, and the wonderful people at Krause who helped to make this book a reality. Thanks to my editor, Christine Townsend, and layout artist Jamie Martin. Many thanks also to Ross Hubbard for photographing the sweaters, and my deepest appreciation to the lovely models, Tracy Schmidt, Amy Tincher-Durik, Jean Stockwell, Alicia LaCanne, Tracy Radies, Tricia Kertzman, and Katherine Stephani. My thanks also to the proprietors of the Green Fountain Inn in Waupaca, Wisconsin, for their hospitality.

The software used to create the graphs is Stitch Crafts Gold©, Version 5, by Compucrafts, P.O. Box 6326, Lincoln Center, Massachusetts. Illustrations were accomplished using Adobe® Illustrator® 8.

Most of the yarns used in this book are from Webs, Division of Valley Fibers Corporation, P.O. Box 147, Northampton, Massachusetts, supplier of Webs' branded yarns, and mill ends. Thanks to Barbara for her invaluable assistance and for graciously supplying yarns.

TABLE OF CONTENTS

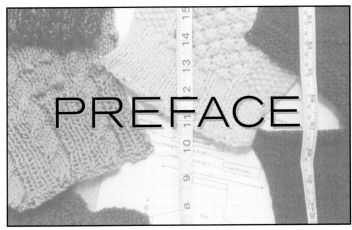

PREFACE

This book, for me, represents a lifetime of knitting experience. Early on, I taught myself how to hold the needles and form the stitches into the shape of a garment. Later, when teaching knitting to others, I had the pleasure of re-learning my own beginnings of this craft! It is truly a joy to be writing about something that has been with me for so many years.

As much as I loved to knit, the ability to make a sweater that I could enjoy wearing eluded me for a long time. Commercial patterns gave no guidelines for getting a sweater to fit right—sleeves were often too constricting, necklines didn't feel right, or instructions were incorrect or incomprehensible, and so on. In short, I made many sweaters that have since been donated to worthy causes, or ripped out and the yarn reused.

In all of my pattern following, there didn't seem to be a remedy for getting a sweater to fit right. The yarn I believed in when I purchased it, and still did even after making a sweater that I couldn't wear. I realized that my difficulties had nothing to do with the yarn, but did have everything to do with the fit of the finished garment.

The revelation came when I first tried to design a sweater. I began by determining the basic shape of a sweater, and then applied my own adaptations to that shape. This was a challenge because I had no set of directives telling me how to proceed, and the sweater patterns of the time were in written form only. There were no diagrams to show the shapes and sizes of the individual parts.

The Russian Jacket was my first original creation. It was knitted after I did sketches and diagrams of my ideas using existing sweaters to check fit and size, and swatches of stitch patterns to find a suitable one for the yarn. Much to my surprise, the sweater turned out perfectly, and is one I still wear. After that first sweater, I have made only original sweaters using the same designing methods; I am truly happy with them, and wear them all regularly.

That very same design process is the one presented in this book, along with the simple tools I have developed to make sweater designing easier. Now you can knit from scratch, or just be more knowledgeable in following patterns to knit sweaters that will give you long-lasting pleasure and pride.

Planning a sweater begins with making swatches to find a suitable pattern stitch.

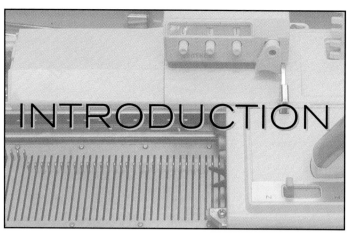

INTRODUCTION

The three main categories for making the sweater of your dreams are:

- Yarn, gauges, and swatches
- Stitch and color patternings
- Instructions for shaping and fitting a sweater

Choose a beautiful yarn; purchase a sufficient quantity—and then what? You are now at a point of beginning, and one of no return. So many really beautiful yarns are available to us, that yarn shopping can seem like going to heaven. Getting the yarn to take the shape of a garment that is equally luscious to wear can be a challenge that keeps knitters from progressing with confidence in their skills. But no more! There are ways to design a garment that include finding the appropriate fit and style, and ways of working with sweater shapes that will result in the sweater of your dreams.

Making a swatch is sometimes the *last* thing we want to do before diving into a new yarn and sweater pattern or idea … but it is the most important thing to do. Swatches teach us about the yarn, and are necessary in obtaining a gauge, and finding the correct needle size. In learning to do designs of your own, you will make many swatches in your exploration of pattern stitches, and in "trying out" new yarns and knitting fibers.

Watching patternings form out of a very few basic stitches is fascinating; there is limitless variety in what can be done with stitches. Learning to "read" patterns from the knitting itself is a simple skill requiring a little observation. After reading through this book and practicing, you will be able to understand how stitch patterns work, and then design your own.

Fitting a sweater has everything to do with what, in terms of clothing, makes you feel most comfortable. The historical use of a sweater has been to provide insulation, to keep warm in the face of plummeting temperatures and chilling winds. Now, sweaters are an integral component of fashion, fitting into any occasion from casual to evening wear, and for all seasons. Regardless of the purpose of the sweater, however, we still need to be comfortable. Getting a sweater to fit well takes only a little planning, and is easy to do.

This book is for all knitters, from beginner to experienced. If you are a beginner, this book will help you to better understand knitting patterns, and gives instructions for basic sweater types. The experienced knitter who wants to be less dependent upon patterns, or do entirely original ideas, is here given direction in doing just that. How to fit and shape a sweater, how to make and evaluate a swatch, and how stitches are made into patterns are the three essential aspects of sweater design. It's easy to get started with any of these.

What to Look for in a Design

Here are a few things to consider as you think about designing a beautiful sweater.

Color

Using a mirror, hold your choice of yarn up to your face. Is it a color you can wear? Does it complement and highlight your skin tones and hair color? Will it fit in with your wardrobe? Is the color in line with most of the clothing colors you already have?

Or, if it is wildly different, are you willing to make that difference in your life? In other words, only bring home the most radiant of the yarn colors from the store if you know that you can and will step out your door in the finished garment. You may consider buying only one skein of that wonderfully brilliant shade, and the remainder in a color you know you are definitely going to wear. Then, use the bright skein sparingly in a color-worked pattern in the sweater.

Texture

Yarn textures vary widely from silky smooth, to coarser, traditional knitting wools and cottons, to fanciful "fuzzies" and chenilles. Fancy pattern stitches show up best in smooth yarns. More textured yarns thrive on simple stitches such as stockinette, reverse stockinette, or garter stitch.

Different weights of yarn affect the appearance of a sweater. In general, heavier yarns such as worsted and bulky weights tend to make a casual sweater with more body and less drape. Finer yarns make a thinner fabric with more drape and less body.

Style

Do you want to knit a traditional style of sweater, or are you looking for something different? The easy way to begin working with styles is to start with the form of a traditional sweater, and work variations into it. You can choose among sleeve styles, ease, types of neckline, pullover versus cardigan, hem treatments, and so on.

At the same time, be willing to experiment, seeking combinations that are interesting, offbeat—or even flashy—whatever it is that reflects who you are.

Comfort

Being comfortable in a sweater has to do with the amount of ease allowed, and the lengths of the different parts of the sweater. The best way to be sure you are making the proper fit for your needs is to find an existing sweater or sweatshirt that fits the way you like it to, measure it, and apply the measurements to your new project.

You may find that as soon as you've finished one sweater that you really love to wear, you'll have an idea for the fit of the next one. You may want to try one that is longer, shorter, wider, or narrower.

Using a Knitting Machine

I sometimes like to make a sweater in a very fine gauge. Hand knitting a fine-gauged sweater is very time-consuming, so I often prefer to use a knitting machine. This way it is possible to start and finish a sweater in as little as one weekend.

Machine knitting is distinctly different from hand knitting. The machine stitch tends to be firmer and very even. The yarns are on cones instead of skeins. The machine itself can appear daunting to a beginner, can take some time to learn, and is far more costly than a set of hand knitting needles.

Although there are no "machine knitting" instructions in this book, the procedure is the same. Make a gauge swatch according to instructions with your machine. Do the *Measuring for Fit* worksheet in this book (page 47), fill the dimensions into the worksheet for the type of sweater you want to knit, and then use the gauge swatch to determine the number of stitches to use. Machine knit the pieces of the sweater, and then sew them together.

A knitting machine adds to the range of possibilities in creating knitwear.

Using a Spinning Wheel

I enjoy creating my own yarns, and this means either actually spinning raw wool, or just plying two or more existing yarns together. I often take two or three fine yarns that were coned for machine knitting, and spin them into a heavier yarn for hand knitting. In this way it is possible to combine textures and colors for many different effects.

Yarns can also be held together while they are knitted. Spinning them results in a more even blending of the fibers that is easier to knit with.

The ideas in this book are readily applicable to hand-spun yarns. Just follow the instructions to create a sweater as unique as the yarn you've spun!

Fine machine knitting yarns can be plied into one heavier yarn by using a spinning wheel or by simply holding them together.

Enjoy the tactile experience of knitting by trying different types of yarns and fibers.

TOOLS

It is a real plus to have a set of knitting needles in all sizes (especially sizes 4 through 10-1/2) in 14" lengths; that way, you can readily change to a different size if you need to. Purchase circulars as needed, (unless you buy them as a set). Circulars are necessary for knitting wide sweaters such as the dolman style, and may be used for neckline ribbings. A large, dull sewing needle is needed for sewing the sweater together. You will need a scissors or trimmers for cutting the yarn.

Have plenty of needles on hand so you always have the size needed.

Other things you will need are:

Tape Measure

Questions of size are resolved by measuring. Always have a tape measure handy, keeping it with your knitting.

Ruler

Important for accurate measuring of gauge swatches.

Calculator

An excellent tool for the minimal number crunching to be done.

Pencil and Eraser

Graph Paper

Regular graph paper, or knitter's graph paper—see Appendix (page 141) or a cross-stitch or knitting computer program. This is for plotting stitch and color patterns, raglan, and other sweater shapings.

Notebook

With lined or unlined paper. Use this for sketching your sweater ideas, and for logging the dimensions, gauges, and stitch patterns of each sweater you knit.

CHAPTER 1
THE YARN OF YOUR CHOICE

The most I can do here is to give some very general information about fibers, as fibers and yarns really are hands-on types-of-things that you need to experience by, and for, yourself: Try the different types of yarns available, make lots of swatches in different stitch patterns, play, experiment, mix different fibers together to get to know their characteristics. Fibers, most especially the natural ones, are wonderful, beautiful things, and they are what knitting is all about. Explore them and luxuriate in them. Learn about them with the awareness that there is always more to be learned.

There are many different types of yarns available that are derived from several basic fibers. These yarns are smooth or textured, nubby, loopy, or shaggy, and yet others are woven ribbons or chenilles. In some yarns the fiber is barely spun, in others it is tightly spun. Some yarns are one-ply; others are two- or more plies (a "ply" is one spun strand of yarn).

Discover the characteristics of the yarn by knitting it. Make swatches of it in stockinette stitch and various pattern stitches. Evaluate the swatches. Check for drape by holding a swatch up by one corner and then laying it over your arm—will it cascade in soft folds, or is it firmer? Try knitting a knit/purl ribbing stitch to find out if a ribbing will have resiliency. Imagine the yarn as a sweater: what type of design will best enhance the yarn and the pattern stitch?

When making swatches, make each large enough so you can get a good idea of how the sweater fabric will look, act, and feel. Knit them at least 4" square (although larger swatch sizes, between 6" and 8", are preferable).

KNITTING FIBERS

Wool

Wool is a classic, time-honored sweater fiber, and the most resilient of the knitting fibers. Individual strands of wool vary in length and curl from one breed of sheep to another … some are coarse, others fine and soft. The breed differences result in yarns that carry those same characteristics, but are not always as evident to the hand knitter as they are to the spinner who works directly with the fleece. Wool is an insulator, so is perfect for winter or any cool-weather wear. Wool loves to be washed, and should always be washed before storing, or moths can be attracted.

By knitting swatches, a pattern stitch can be found that is appropriate for the yarn. The two yarns here are a yellow alpaca and a multi-colored cotton.

Cotton and Linen

Cotton and linen are both plant fibers, but they are processed in ways that are very different from each other. Cotton grows on the plant as a ball of fluff that is then picked, processed, and spun. Linen is spun from strands of fiber that are taken from the stem of the flax plant after a long process ("retting") that rots away the unusable parts of it. Both fibers lack resiliency, but are excellent for summer knitwear, and are washable in any water temperature.

Rayon

Rayon is a machine-made fiber derived from wood or cottonseed, kind of a hybrid of both "natural" and "synthetic." Rayon can be slippery-smooth and highly lustrous, but can also be made to have a matte finish. Like cottons, rayons are not resilient. Weightier than wool, the knitted fabric is often very drapey, and is wonderful for making elegant sweaters. Rayon is washable in cool water, but the fiber weakens when wet so it should be washed with care (it firms up when dried).

Silk

Silk is made from silkworm cocoons that are either unraveled, or carded and spun. Many of its qualities are similar to rayon, except it is the lightest-weight of fibers. Pure silk has a dry, crunchy feel, distinguishing it from synthetics. Silk can be both warm and elegant, has excellent drape, and is wonderful when blended with fibers such as wool or cotton. Wash silks gently in cool to lukewarm water.

Acrylic

Acrylics are washable, synthetic wool-substitutes that are excellent for children's wear, or for those who are allergic to wool.

Angora/Cashmere/Mohair/Alpaca

These are specialty fibers. Angora is from the Angora rabbit, and makes a very soft and lightly fuzzy yarn. Mohair comes from a goat, and makes a very fuzzy, or fuzzy and loopy, yarn that is coarser than angora. Cashmere is a smooth goat fiber, making a luxuriously soft yarn. Alpaca is made from the wool of a South American mammal that is related to llamas. Alpaca is similar to wool, but is softer and very warm.

Synthetics

In addition to acrylics, there are the synthetics that sometimes make up the entire yarn, but are often used in addition to natural fibers in blended yarns. These can be of any description—smooth, fuzzy, loopy, metallic and so on. Follow the care instructions that come with these yarns.

YARN SIZES, APPROXIMATE GAUGES, AND NEEDLE SIZES

Yarns, whatever the fiber, are classified by how thick they are, and these sizes are called "weights," as you can see in the chart. There are also in-between sizes. Most skeined yarns are labeled with a suggested needle size and the stitch gauge that can be expected. The stitch gauge refers to stockinette stitch; the same yarn used in a fancy pattern stitch is likely to have a very different gauge.

You can see that a yarn that obtains a gauge of three stitches to the inch requires fewer stitches to be knitted than, say, a yarn that knits to eight stitches per inch. The heavier yarns make heavier sweaters that are quicker to knit. The lighter-weight yarns make softer, drapier sweaters that take longer to knit.

From bottom to top: fingering weight yarn on size 4 needles, sport weight yarn on 6's, worsted weight yarn on 8's, and bulky weight on 10-1/2's.

Fingering weight	7–8 sts	= 1"	Needles 2–4
Sport weight	6–7 sts	= 1"	Needles 5–7
Worsted weight	4–5.5 sts	= 1"	Needles 7–9
Bulky weight	3–3.75 sts	= 1"	Needles 10–11

CHOOSING THE CORRECT NEEDLE SIZE

If you have chosen a yarn that is not labeled with an appropriate needle size, or if you have spun or plied to create your own yarn, you will need to find the needle size on your own. Choose a needle size—guess at what is close to a correct size—and knit a swatch perhaps 4" (10 cm) square. You may need to knit several swatches using different size needles each time, then compare them.

Evaluate the swatch. Look for the knitting to be springy but not baggy, and firm but not constricted. If the knitting turns out baggy, the sweater will not hold its shape. If the knitting is constricted, the sweater may feel stiff and unpliable, and will take longer to knit than if you "up" the needle size. Look for additional characteristics that will affect how the sweater will feel when it is worn. Fuzzy mohairs, for instance, can be too warm and dense if knitted tightly.

KNITTING A GAUGE SWATCH

Knit a swatch at least 4" (10 cm) square (or larger, if necessary) to include a full repeat of any pattern stitch used. Bind off, and lay it out flat. If it curls, pin the edges to an ironing board or other pin-able surface.

Using a ruler, find the number of inches that give a whole number, such as 2" over nine stitches. You will then need to divide to find the exact number of stitches per inch. Nine divided by two inches = 4-1/2 stitches per inch. I always re-measure in another area, and measure the width of the swatch itself, and then compare the results to check for accuracy.

If the per-inch gauge is fractional, use that exact number (it can be rounded to a number plus two decimals) in figuring how many stitches to knit.

Find the row gauge by measuring vertically and counting the rows per inch.

If the sweater will be blocked (see Blocking, page 15), block the gauge swatch and measure for the gauge after blocking.

PREPARING A SWATCH WHEN USING CONED YARNS

Yarns that are skeined for hand knitting do not require any pre-treatment. I frequently use yarns that are coned for machine knitting. These yarns are often wound on the cones rather firmly and may change after washing as the yarn relaxes. Knit the gauge swatch, then wash, dry, and block the swatch exactly as will be done with the finished sweater, then measure for the gauge. Wash, dry, and block the sweater pieces before sewing them together.

ESTIMATING YARDAGE

Most yarn labels include the weight of the yarn, and the yardage of the skein. The weights of yarn vary widely, since weight depends on type of fiber, number of plies, and how tightly or loosely the yarn is spun. Unless we are using only one brand and style of yarn, the weight of the yarn cannot be used to determine how much is needed.

Using the yardage is a more accurate way of determining the amount needed. Yarn shops can often give an estimate of the yardage needed to make a sweater of a particular size. If, however, your idea includes extra length and width, or a yarn-consuming pattern stitch, it will be necessary to do your own calculations. (Note: if using metrics, use meters instead of yards.)

Using a couple of pins make it easy to discern the number of stitches per inch.

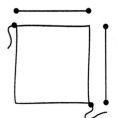

1. Knit a swatch 4" (10cm) to 8" (20cm) square or larger, as needed, to encompass any pattern stitches used. On paper, make a note of the size of the swatch. Now rip it out.

2. Lay a tape measure out flat. Without stretching the yarn, measure the yarn from the ripped-out swatch (one yard is 36"). Jot down the number of yards, then find the yardage per square inch as follows:

Yardage divided by square inches = yards per square inch.
Example:
Yardage swatch of 4" square = 16 square inches.
Ripped out yardage = 10.5 yards.
10.5 divided by 16 = .66 yards per square inch.

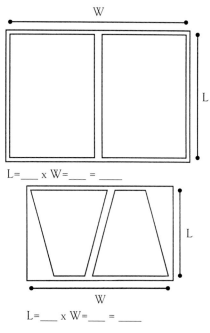

3. Sketch the pieces of your sweater design so they are laid inside of rectangular areas. Write in the lengths and widths of the rectangles. Multiply the length times the width of each of the areas and add them together (you will need to estimate somewhat). Now, multiply the total square inches of the sweater pieces by the yards per square inch obtained in Step 2, above. This gives the approximate number of yards needed to knit the sweater. Add a little extra to cover the ribbings, and do buy an extra skein just in case. Unused skeins can usually be returned, but you can also keep them, and use small amounts in color-worked designs.

RIPPING OUT

The nature of designing is that it is a trial-and-error process. There will be a need to rip out sections, and even whole pieces, of your knitting. It's always best to take it out if it isn't right. After you've ripped out a few times, you get used to doing it, and accept it as part of knitting.

While we are on the subject, begin ripping out the sweaters you have made but haven't worn. Prepare the yarn for re-knitting by winding it into loose skeins and washing it. Allow the yarn to dry—you may need to weight it to get the kinks out—then wind it into loose balls. Think about what you would rather make out of the yarn, and sketch some ideas. My own policy is that if I haven't worn a sweater once in a full year, there must be something I don't like about it. Time to rip!

Pick up stitches from the row below so none are lost.

Tip:

Sometimes you will need to rip out a section of your knitting to correct a mistake or make a change. Here is an accurate method of picking up the stitches so they do not become twisted or lost. Rip out all of the rows that need to be removed except one. A stitch at a time, carefully tug on the unraveling yarn and, as the stitch is about to pop loose, pick it up on a knitting needle without twisting the stitch.

If you are only taking out one row, keep the stitches on the needle and hold it in your left hand (reverse for left-handedness). Insert the other needle into the stitch below the unwanted row on the left-hand needle, slide the stitch off the left needle, pull out the unwanted stitch, and continue across the row. This is especially useful if you are knitting a fancy pattern stitch and need to keep the integrity of the stitches. Yarn-overs and other stitches can easily become lost in ripping out.

WASHING

Always check yarn labels before washing or blocking. Some yarns must be dry cleaned, and some should not be blocked.

Any washable yarn can be washed according to these guidelines for washing wool. You will notice there is no agitation in this recipe—do not agitate your wool sweater or it will "felt." Felting tends to erase the lines between individual stitches of the knitting, making the surface into a smooth, fuzzy blur. Fibers other than wool can be moved about in the water, although it really isn't necessary if you use this soaking technique. Also, wool shrinks if subjected to differing water temperatures, and if heated while drying.

Use cool water, staying with the same temperature throughout the process if you are washing wool. Fill a basin with water and add a mild soap. Place the sweater into the water. Allow it to soak for awhile (I leave mine for several hours because I tend to forget it's there). Pull the plug and let the water drain. Again, walk away so it can continue to drain as water runs out of the sweater.

Now begin the rinsing. Refill the basin with water (let it fill so the water runs in next to, not on to, the sweater) and let it soak for a few minutes to a few hours depending on your schedule. Pull the plug and let it drain again.

Repeat the rinsing until the rinse water runs clear. Squeeze the sweater very gently to remove any water, then lay it on a bath towel. Wrap the towel around the sweater, and add another towel if needed. Leave it to lie until the towels are soggy; you can repeat this step using dry towels if needed.

Now the sweater can be draped over a drying rack or several clotheslines so it is well supported. Dry it away from heat or sun. The best time to launder sweaters is on a cool, breezy day when they can be dried in the shade outdoors. You will find that once dried, the sweater will have regained its original shape and it will smell like fresh wool.

BLOCKING

I have found blocking to be mostly unnecessary. Blocking can be used to correct the sizes of sweater pieces if they were knitted incorrectly, or if they somehow stretched out in knitting (neither of these things should happen). Be sure to check first with the label of the yarn, because some yarns should not be blocked.

Some knitters love to block, so if this is your forte, here is how. The easiest way is to pin the sweater piece out flat and then lightly mist with water, and leave it alone until it is completely dried. When pinning, measure to check that lengths and widths are as intended.

Blocking can also be achieved by steaming. Pin the piece, cover it with a bath towel, and move a steam iron in circles over the towel (without touching it). Remove the towel and leave the knitted piece to dry.

Use any pin-able surface that won't be damaged by water. I use a large, well-stuffed floor pillow made of velveteen.

I use a velvet floor pillow for blocking—whatever works!

CHAPTER 2

THE
PATTERNS
OF
STITCHES

The idea of this chapter is not to provide a stitch dictionary, but to show how stitch patterns can be created. By following along with the order of the patterns (they grow in complexity), and by knitting them, you should begin to see how to design your own. Use the pattern examples as jumping off points for your own ideas, and think up ways to work variations on them.

You can also do what I've done here: make same-size swatches of all of the stitch patterns and sew them together into an afghan. The afghan can then serve as a visual "dictionary" of stitches.

Observe your knitting as you work the stitch patterns. Learn to "read" the knitting so you can always see where you are in a pattern, and you will then be able to follow the pattern in that way. This is also important if you wish to devise your own stitch patterns, and in combining several patterns into one sweater. After knitting a swatch, turn it over and look at the back of it—you may be looking at yet another stitch pattern idea.

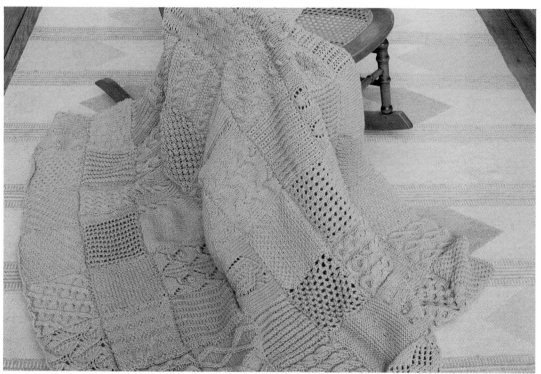

Make same-size swatches of the stitch patterns and sew them together to make an afghan. This is a good exercise in establishing gauges—you will need to find the gauge for each stitch pattern in order to make the swatch a particular size. The blocks in this afghan are 6-1/2" square.

Tips:

In following some stitch patterns, keeping track of which is the right side of the knitting can be difficult. When you begin knitting, on a right-side row, observe where the "tail" is (the beginning of the yarn), either to the left or the right of the knitting. If you remember where it is, then you will always know you are working on the right or wrong side of the knitting.

If you set your knitting down in the middle of a row, it is easy to find which way to continue. Look for where the yarn is coming from. That's where you knitted last, and now you need to continue the yarn onto the other needle.

The swatches shown on the following pages were knitted in worsted weight yarn on size 9 needles. Other weights and types of yarns, and choice of needle size, may give a different appearance from what is seen in the photos.

Stitch patterns are affected by the type of yarn that is used. Some yarns will show a pattern distinctly, while others will blur pattern textures to varying degrees. "Ya never know 'til ya try it," is the axiom I go by. The only way to discover what works best is by making lots of swatches trying different patterns. Here are some suggestions for different types of yarns:

- Smooth yarns—try the knit/purl combinations or any stitch pattern.
- Light to medium textured yarns—try any pattern stitch, use what works best.
- Heavily textured yarns—plain stitches such as stockinette, reverse stockinette, or garter stitch.
- Mohair—bold cables or other bold patterns.
- Smooth, lightweight yarns—lace, or intricate patterns.
- Bulky yarns—cables or bold patterns that use simple stitches.

READING GRAPHED STITCH PATTERNS

Begin reading a graphed pattern at the bottom of the graph. Row 1 is (usually) the right side (RS) of the knitting, and is read from right to left. Row 2 is the wrong side (WS), and is read from left to right. Repeat the rows in the same sequence.

Each square represents one stitch of one row. Refer to the Symbol Definitions on the inside covers of the book to be sure how to work each stitch.

Graphed designs are more than representations of stitches to follow; they also give a "picture" of the design. In knit/purl, color, lace, and cable designs you can see from the graph how the stitches will appear in the knitting. In knit/purl patterns, as well as color patterns, by drawing on graph paper several repeats of a pattern you can see what the effect will be on a sweater. In lace patterns, the placement of the YO's shows where the holes will appear. In cables, you can see where, and how often, the cabling occurs.

DESIGNING AND GRAPHING STITCH PATTERNS

Once you've learned to read a graphed design, the next step is to learn to design your own stitch and color patterns. Designs can be invented by doodling on graph paper. Use the symbols that have the most meaning for you (symbols are often different from one designer to another).

When I graph stitch pattern ideas, I try to keep the design as simple as possible. For instance, in knit/purl patterns, it is easiest to knit a design in which the reverse side row repeats the stitches of the right side row (knit a stitch on the right side, purl it on the wrong side). In patterns featuring several cables, having all of the cables cross in the same row makes it easy to keep track of when to cable. In lace patterns, it is easiest to work all of the "lace-making" stitches on the right side, and to purl the entire reverse side row. It isn't always possible to simplify as much as this, but thinking of ways to make the knitting easier, quicker, or more intuitive is well worth doing.

Ordinary graph paper does not accurately represent knitting. In knitting, there are often more rows than stitches to the inch. Take this into consideration by adding an extra row here and there, making the pattern appear elongated vertically. You can also use knitter's graph paper—the squares are wider than they are long. By knitting a swatch of the design, you will be able to see if any adjustments need to be made. See page 141 for knitter's graph paper

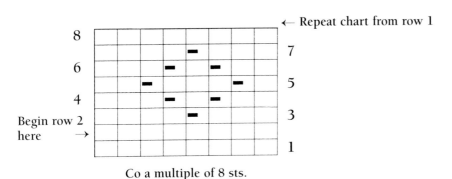

Co a multiple of 8 sts.

MULTIPLES AND STITCH GAUGES

A "multiple" is the basis of a stitch or color pattern. If the "base" stitches are repeated across a row, the design is continuous.

Cast on a number that divides to the multiple in order to have an even number of repeats of the pattern. For instance, a multiple of 4 requires a number of stitches evenly divisible by 4: 8, 16, 20, 24, 28, 32, and so on.

A multiple applies to one stitch or color pattern. Two or more pattern repeats can be combined to form one multiple. For instance, one design may be a repeat of two stitches, and another consists of four stitches repeating. The multiple to use is four, because it encompasses both designs (add the repeats together). Most of the stitch patterns are presented as "multiples," with the graph showing only one repeat. For instance, if the same three stitches are repeated, the multiple is three. Base your sweater on the stitch multiple. Make the back and front pieces a number of stitches that divide to that number, and begin the sleeves using it. That way, the design will run continuously around the body of the sweater, and will be centered on the sleeves.

Use the multiple and the stitch gauge in combination to determine the number of stitches to knit a sweater. For example: Your stitch gauge tells you to use 86 stitches for each of the front and back pieces for the size of sweater you want to knit. The stitch pattern that you've chosen has a multiple of five stitches. 86 divided by 5 = 17.2. You need a whole number, so round the answer down to 17, or up to 18 repeats of the design. 17 x 5 = 85 sts. 18 x 5 = 90 sts. Use either 85 or 90 stitches to knit the sweater.

In working with copies of a design, try as many different arrangements as you can think of, spacing the foreground objects closer together or farther apart, or stacking them, and observe how they relate to each other and how the background changes in relation to the design. I call this process "taking a design through its paces," and find it to be a necessary step in discovering the best way a design will work.

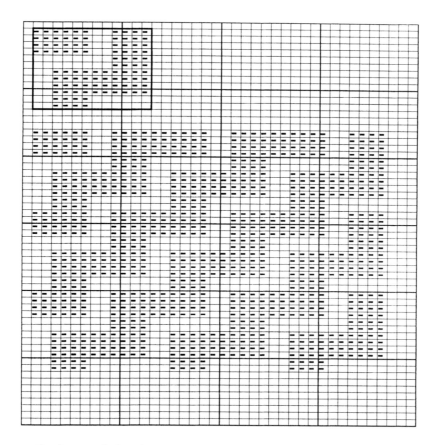

This design, in the boxed area at the top, was copied a number of times both horizontally and vertically to see how it would look on a sweater.

Here, a floral design was mirrored, then copied six times. Note how the background creates a secondary design. Focus your eyes on the spaces between the floral shapes to see this.

The same floral desing, in different arrangements.

Tip:

A computer program is quicker, neater, and easier to use than graph paper. The cross-stitch program I use has plenty of symbols that can be used as is (or edited), and the graph can be modified to reflect a greater number of rows-to-the-inch than stitches. Knitting programs work much the same way. Here are the advantages to using a computer program:

Erasing is clean and instantaneous (erasing is an inevitable part of designing).

A design can be copied, and the copy can be worked on so as to keep the original intact.

Designs can be mirrored both vertically and horizontally (see the floral design on facing page).

A design can be copied and pasted to make enough repeats to show how it will look on a sweater.

A design can be printed in the size needed. Very complicated designs are easier to read if enlarged, and simple designs, in which only a few set-up rows are needed, can be printed in a smaller size.

Although the software makes all of these things both quick and simple to do, I also often do a preliminary sketch on plain or graph paper. Find what works best for you by trying the different ways.

KNIT AND PURL PATTERNS

Knit/purl pattern stitches make use of the "bump" of the purl stitch on a stockinette stitch background, or the reverse—the lack of bumps on a reverse stockinette stitch ground. Note how the variations of the patterns change the texture of the knitted fabric. It sometimes only takes a slight variation to create an entirely different effect.

Directions for the variations are not written out, but can be followed in the graphs. Multiples for the variations are shown by the number of stitches enclosed in the box around the graph.

In the written instructions, the asterisks (*) show the part of the design that is repeated. *Repeat between the *'s until the end of the row unless directed otherwise.* Where the instruction simply says "K" or "P," knit or purls the entire row. Where parts of an instruction appear in (parentheses) do that part the number of times indicated, then move on: "(C4F) twice, K4" means to cable over 4 stitches two times, then K4.

Repeat the sequence of rows in order unless directed otherwise.

THE THREE MOST BASIC STITCHES USED FOR KNITTING SWEATERS

Garter Stitch

Notice this fabric is thicker than that of stockinette stitch, and that the edges do not curl, making it good for sweater edges. It makes a dense fabric that is thicker than stockinette stitch.
Row 1 K
Row 2 K

Garter stitch.

Stockinette Stitch

This is the most-used stitch in sweater-knitting.
Row 1 K
Row 2 P

Stockinette stitch.

Reverse Stockinette

This is also the reverse side of the stockinette stitch.
Row 1: P
Row 2: K

Reverse stockinette.

Seed Stitch

mult of 2

Variations: Space the "seeds" farther apart, and/or add more plain rows in between.
Row 1: * K1, P1 *
Row 2: P
Row 3: * P1, K1 *
Row 4: P

Seed stitch.

Seed stitch.

Seed stitch.

☐ **K on RS, P on WS**   ⊟ **P on RS, K on WS**

22

Moss Stitch

mult of 2

    This pattern comes out the same on front and back. Variation: make a "thicker" moss by doubling up on the stitches.

Row 1: * K1, P1 *
Row 2: * P1, K1 *

Moss stitch.

Moss stitch.

Diamond Pattern

mult of 5

    Seed stitches are placed to form diamond-like shapes.

    Variations: make the diamond shapes larger or more pronounced.

Row 1: K
Rows 2 and 6: P
Row 3: * K2, P1, K2 *
Row 4: * (P1, K1) twice, P1 *
Row 5: same as Row 3
Rep rows 1 - 6

Diamond pattern.

Diamond pattern.

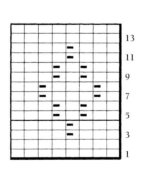

Diamond pattern.

Diamond pattern.

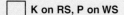 

Diagonal Pattern

mult of 5

Variations: reverse the diagonal at intervals to make a zigzag pattern, or make the pattern more pronounced.

Row 1: * K4, P1 *
Row 2: * P1, K1, P3 *
Row 3: * K2, P1, K2 *
Row 4: * P3, K1, P1 *
Row 5: * K1, P4 *

Continue as established, moving the P stitch one stitch over on the right side, and moving the K stitch one stitch over on the wrong side rows.

Diagonal pattern.

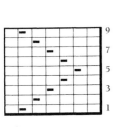

Diagonal pattern.

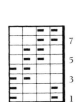

Diagonal pattern.

Block Pattern

mult of 8

Variations: make the blocks larger or smaller, or in varied sizes. Rows 1 and 3: * K4, P4 *
Rows 2 and all WS rows: P the knit, and K the purl stitches of previous row.
Rows 5 and 7: * P4, K4 *
Rep rows 1 - 8

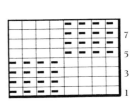

Block pattern.

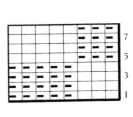

Block pattern.

Triangle Blocks

mult of 6
Row 1: * K5, P1 *
Row 2: * P2, K4 *
Row 3: * K3, P3 *
Row 4: * P4, K2 *
Row 5: * K1, P5 *
Row 6: K

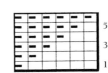

Triangle blocks.

K on RS, P on WS   — P on RS, K on WS

Geometric Designs

Geometric patterns are easy to design on graph paper. The diagram shows only one repeat of the design shown. Knit the design by following the graph.

Geometric designs.

Non-geometric Designs

Floral and other forms can be worked into knit/purl patterns. Look around you for ideas to graph, then try them by knitting them. The possibilities are endless. I prefer floral forms, but all around us are numerous shapes that can be tried. Larger designs such as these are easiest to knit by following the graph. Writing out the patterns would be arduous.

Non-geometric designs.

Non-geometric designs.

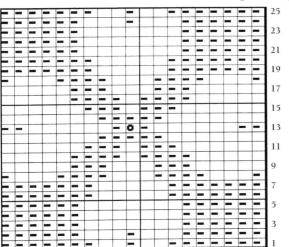

 K on RS, P on WS   P on RS, K on WS   ⭘ Bobble

RIBBINGS

Any stitch pattern that creates a narrow column-like effect can be classified as a ribbing. Most often used along the edges of knitwear, ribbings form sturdy edges that don't curl. Often ribbings are used to "draw in" the sweater so it fits snugly around your hips, wrists, and neck. The stretchiest type of ribbing for this purpose is the knit/purl rib, in its various combinations of 1 x 1 (Knit 1, Purl 1), 2 x 1, 2 x 2, and so on.

The fiber used also has an effect on the ribbing. Wool gives the most springiness in combination with a knit/purl rib. The same ribbing worked in cotton, for instance, will have less stretch because the cotton fiber lacks elasticity.

Experiment with various combinations of knit and purl stitches, trying other combinations than those given here such as 3 x 2, 4 x 2, 5 x 2, 5 x 3, and so on.

1 x 1 Ribbing

mult of 2
Row 1: * K1, P1 *
Row 2: same as row 1

1 x 1 ribbing, multiple of two.

4 x 3 Ribbing

mult of 7
Row 1: * K4, P3 *
Row 2: * K3, P4 *

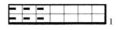

4 x 3 ribbing, multiple of seven.

2 x 2 Ribbing

mult of 4
Row 1: * K2, P2 *
Row 2: same as row 1

2 x 2 ribbing, multiple of four.

Crossed 2 x 2 Ribbing

mult of 4
Row 1: * C2F, P2 *
Row 2: * K2, P2 *

Crossed 2 x 2 ribbing, multiple of four.

2 x 1 Ribbing

mult of 3
Row 1: * K2, P1 *
Row 2: * K1, P2 *

2 x 1 ribbing, multiple of three.

Crossed 2 x 1 Ribbing

mult of 3
Row 1: * C2B, P1 *
Row 2: * K1, P2 *

Crossed 2 x 1 ribbing, multiple of three.

 K on RS, P on WS  P on RS, K on WS   C2F   C2B

Broken Ribbing

mult of 3
Row 1: K
Row 2: * K2, P1 *

Broken ribbing, multiple of three.

Twisted Ribs

There are two ways to do a twisted rib. The twisted stitches can be worked on the right side only. Or, the twisted stitch is twisted on the right side, and again on the wrong side. Twisting on the right side only creates a textured stitch, while twisting on both sides makes a firmer stitch.

Twisted 1 x 1 Ribbing

mult of 2
Row 1: * K1B, P1 *
Row 2: * K1, P1 (or P1B) *

Twisted 1 x 1 ribbing, multiple of two.

Twisted 2 x 1 Ribbing

mult of 3
Row 1: * K1B (twice), P1 *
Row 2: K1, P2 (or P1B
    twice) *

Twisted 2 x 1 ribbing, multiple of three.

Chunky 1 x 1 Ribbing

mult of 2
   Knitting into the stitch below the one on the needle creates a thicker, larger stitch.
Rows 1, 2, and 4: * K1, P1 *
Row 3: * K1 into stitch
    below, P1 *
Rep rows 3 and 4

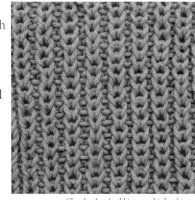

Chunky 1 x 1 ribbing, multiple of two.

Garter and Rib

mult of 9
   Note that this stitch gives a shaped edge to the knitting.
Row 1: * K3, (P1, K1) 3
    times *
Row 2: * (P1, K1) 3 times,
    K3 *

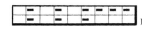

Garter and rib.

Moss and Rib

mult of 8
Row 1: * K1, P1 *
Row 2: * P1, K1, (K1, P1)
    3 times *

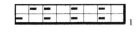

Moss and rib.

Cable Ribbing

mult of 9
Row 1: * K1, P1, K4, P1,
    K1, P1 *
Row 2: * K1, P1, K1, P4,
    K1, P1 *
Row 3: * K1, P1, C4B, P1,
    K1, P1 *
Row 4: same as row 2
Rep rows 1 - 4

Cable rib.

| 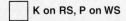 K on RS, P on WS |  P on RS, K on WS | K1B on RS, P1B on WS |  K into st below | C4B |

Colorful ribbings: the two at the top of the photograph are corrugated ribbings—work the K sts in one color, and the P stitches in a second color stranding the unused color across the back. The bottom two are worked two or more rows in one color, then two or more rows in a second color.

CABLES

The principle of cabling is simple: The designated stitches are crossed over each other, the procedure being completed within one row of knitting. You will need a cable needle (or any similar device—I often use a hairpin or a paper clip unfolded into the shape of a hairpin) to temporarily hold the few stitches that are being cabled.

There are four basic types of cables: Rope, double, uncrossed, and traveling. In rope cables, the stitches are crossed over each other in one direction only—either to the right or the left. Double cables have the crossings made in both directions. In uncrossed cables, the cabled stitches do not cross behind other stitches, staying instead on the surface of the knitted fabric. In traveling cables, the cable stitches are moved one stitch at a time to either direction, and are either crossed or not.

Tips for cabling:

Placing the cabled stitches to the back of the work crosses the cable to the right. Bringing the cabled stitches to the front crosses to the left.
Do not twist the cabled stitches as they are placed back onto the needle—keep them in the same order they were already in.
When combining cables in a sweater design, try to match the row repeats so all the cabling is done on the same row. This makes it easy to know when to cable.

Cables worked on a background of stockinette stitch give a different effect than placing purl stitches alongside.

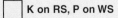 K on RS, P on WS   C4B

Ways to Vary Cables

- Increase or decrease the number of stitches cabled—you can cable 2 (C2F, C2B), 4 (C4F, C4B), 6 (C6F, C6B), 8 (C8F, C8B), and more stitches. The more stitches cabled, the more your garment will be "drawn in." Larger cables decrease the stitch gauge.
- Increase the distance between cable rows by any even number of rows, elongating the cable.
- Work cables with or without purl stitches alongside. Cables can be worked on a background of stockinette or any pattern stitch.
- Rope cables are traditionally made using an even number of stitches, but can be done on uneven stitch counts. (To cable five sts, place two on cn, hold to front or back of work, K3, K2 from cable needle, for example.)
- The open center of traveling cables can be filled with moss, bobbles, or other pattern stitches.
- The cable itself can be worked in other stitches besides the stockinette; try cabling in ribbing and other pattern stitches.

Multiples for the following cables are given only where cables are used in combination with other pattern stitches. Most are given as individual cables, which are often used within other stitch patterns. Often, cables are set apart from the rest of the knitting by placing one or more purl stitches on either side.

Rope Cable 1

worked over 4 sts
Row 1: K4
Row 2 and all WS rows: P
Row 3: C4B
Rep rows 1 - 4

Rope Cable 1

Rope Cable 2

worked over 4 sts
Rows 1 and 5: K4
Row 2 and all WS rows: P
Row 3: C4B
Rep rows 1 - 6.

Rope Cable 2.

Rope Cable 3

Variations can be done simply by deciding on which row to cable.

Rope Cable 3.

Isolated Cable

worked over 8 sts
Small sections of cables can be inserted anywhere in your knitting.
Rows 1 and 5: P2, K4, P2
Rows 2, 4, 6, and 8: P the knit, and K the purl sts of previous row
Rows 3 and 7: P2, C4B, P2

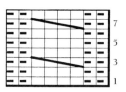

Isolated cable.

Edging Cable

A cable can be knitted all by itself and then used as an edging. C.o. 8 stitches and cable on the fifth row and every eighth row (C8B) after that. After working to the length needed, bind off. On the sample shown here, stitches were picked up along the cable's edge and knitted in stockinette stitch. The cable could also have been sewn on to the edge of a sweater.

Edging cable.

Rope Cable With Moss

mult of 8
Rows 1 and 5: * (K1, P1) twice, K4 *
Row 2 and all WS rows: * P4, (P1, K1) twice *
Row 3: * (K1, P1) twice, C4B *
Rep rows 1 - 6

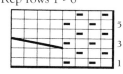

Rope cable with moss.

Rope Cable with Moss Block Pattern

mult of 8

Cables interspersed with blocks of moss stitch create a pattern with a distinctly diagonal feel.
Rows 1, 3, and 7: * (K1, P1) twice, K4 *
Rows 2, 4, and 6: * P4, (P1, K1) twice *
Row 5: * (K1, P1) twice, C4B *
Rows 9, 11 and 15: * K4, (K1, P1) twice *
Rows 10, 12, 14, and 16: * (P1, K1) twice, P4 *
Row13: * C4B, (K1, P1) twice *
Rep rows 1 - 16

Cable and rib.

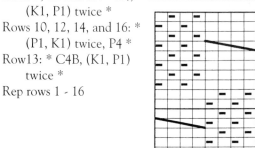

 K on RS, P on WS   — P on RS, K on WS   C4B   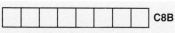 C8B

Cable and Ribbing

mult of 15

Similar to the cable and rib pattern earlier, this is the same on a larger scale. While the other was intended for a ribbed edging, this is suitable for a sweater body.

Row 1 and 3: * K6, (P1, K1) 4 times, P1 *
Row 2: and all WS rows: P the knit, and K the purl stitches of previous row.
Row 5: * C6B, (P1, K1) 4 times, P1 *
Rep rows 1 - 6

Cable and Ribbing

Multiple Plaited Cable

worked over 18 sts

Change the width by adding or subtracting a multiple of 4 stitches. Use as a panel amongst other stitch patterns.

Rows 1 and 5: K18
Row 2 and all WS rows: P
Row 3: (C4F) 4 times, K2
Row 7: K2, (C4B) 4 times
Rep rows 1 - 8

Multiple Plaited Cable

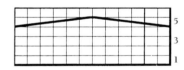

Plaited Cable

worked over 9 sts

A double cable in which the crossings alternate.

Rows 1 and 5: K9
Row 2 and all WS rows: P
Row 3: C6F, K3
Row 7: K3, C6B
Rep rows 1 – 8

Plaited Cable

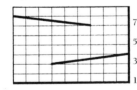

Wishbone Cable

worked over 12 sts

Note in this double cable how the direction of the cables is different from the plaited cable, going outward from the center instead of intertwining.

Rows 1 and 3: K12
Row 2 and all WS rows: P
Row 5: C6B, C6F
Rep rows 1 - 6

Plaited Cable Reversed

Vary the plaited cable by working C6B in place of C6F, and C6F in place of C6B. To see what this looks like, simply turn the above swatch upside down.

Horseshoe Cable

Worked the same as the wishbone cable but the cables are reversed. Work C6F, C6B instead of C6B, C6F. To see what it looks like, turn the wishbone cable upside down.

| | K on RS, P on WS | — | P on RS, K on WS | | C6B | | C6F | | C4B | | C4F |

30

Wave Cable

worked over 4 sts

Cabling creates a sinuous, wavy pattern without crossings.
Rows 1 and 5: K4
Row 2 and all WS rows: P
Row 3: C4B
Row 7: C4F
Rep rows 1 - 8

Wave Cable

XO Cable

worked over 8 sts
Rows 1, 5, 9, and 13: K8
Row 2 and all WS rows: P the knit, and K the purl sts of previous row.
Rows 3 and 7: C4B, C4F
Rows 11, and 15: C4F, C4B
Rep rows 1 - 16

XO Cable

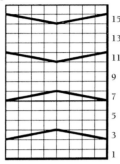

Honeycomb with Rope Cable

mult of 8 + 4

As an example of experimenting with cables, two different types of cable were combined, alternating with each other to create a new and different stitch pattern. Rows 3 and 11 are the two cable rows of honeycomb, and rows 7 and 15 are rope cable.
Rows 1, 5, 9, and 13: K
Row 2 and all WS rows: P
Row 3: K2, * (C4B, C4F,) * end with K2
Row 7: C4B, * (K4, C4B) *
Row 11: K2, * (C4F, C4B) * K2
Row 15: K4, * (C4B, K4) *
Rep rows 1 - 16

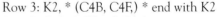

Honeycomb Cable

mult of 8 sts

This is the same idea as the wave cable, placing the cables side by side and alternating the direction of every other cable.
Rows 1 and 5: K
Row 2 and all WS rows: P
Row 3: C4B, C4F
Row 7: C4F, C4B
Rep rows 1 - 8

Honeycomb Cable

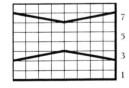

Honeycomb with Rope Cable

No diagram provided; follow the written instructions.

Tips:

Panels Versus Continuous Stitch Patterns

Some designs will result in a half of a part of the design at the sides of the swatch; for instance, the two "knit" stitches in row 3, above, represent half of the four-stitch cable. This design will work fine if the sweater is knitted "in the round," thereby eliminating the half-stitch pattern, or if the pattern stitch is used in a panel surrounded by other pattern stitches. However, if used for an entire sweater front and back, it will show up as an unworked area when the side seams are sewn together.

	K on RS, P on WS		C4B		C4F

Traveling Cable

worked over 12 sts
Row 1: P3, T3B, T3F, P3
Row 2: and all wrong side
   rows: purl the knit,
   and knit the purl
   stitches of previous
   row.
Row 3: P2, T3B, P2, T3F,
   P2
Row 5: P1, T3B, P4, T3F,
   P1
Row 7: T3B, P6, T3F
Row 9: T3F, P6, T3B
Row 11: P1, T3F, P4, T3B,
   P1
Row 13: P2, T3F, P2, T3B,
   P2
Row 15: P3, T3F, T3B, P3
Row 17: P4, C4B, P4
Rep rows 1 - 18

Traveling Cable

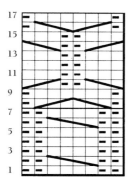

If you get the
impression after working
up this swatch that you
can get cables to "wander"
all over your knitting, you
are right. Begin with a greater number of stitches and establish
several cables on a background of reverse stockinette.
"Wander" them creatively.

Traveling with Rope Cable

worked over 8 sts
   This cable begins on a
WS row.
Rows 1: (WS) K2, P4, K2
Rows 2 and 6: (rs) P2,
   C4B, P2
Row 3 and all WS rows: K
   the purl, and P the
   knit sts of previous
   row.
Row 4: P2, K4, P2
Row 8: P1, T3B, T3F, P1
Row 10: T3B, P2, T3F
Row 12: K3, P2, K3
Row 14: T3F, P2, T3B
Row 16: P1, T3F, T3B, P1
Rep rows 2 - 17

Traveling with Rope Cable

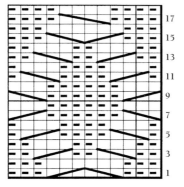

Lacy-textured fabrics can be created by experimenting
with different arrangements of yarn-overs combined with
decrease stitches as in laces 1, 2, and 7. Flat laces are a simple
matter of creating holes in the knitted fabric by using yarn-
overs (see Laces 3 and 4). Other laces are more sculptural and
require more thought, ingenuity, and experimentation to
design. Compare the following graphs to the knitted pieces,
and knit a swatch of each while observing the knitting to see
how the stitches form lace.

Use lace as all-over sweater fabrics, or as panels within
other stitch patterns.

Some of the patterns require an extra stitch at the
beginning or end of rows that is not part of the multiple. And
some patterns have a different number of stitches from one row
to the next—so for the purpose of graphing, where there is no
stitch, the square is blocked out.

Lace 1

mult: an even number of
   stitches
   Compare laces 1 and 2
to see how YO's and K2togs
can be used to create
various patterns.
Row 1: K1, *YO, K2tog, *
   end with K1
Row 2: P1, *YO, P2 tog, *
   end with P1

Lace 1

Lace 2

mult: an uneven number of
   stitches
   This pattern staggers
the stitches just enough to
create a slight zigzag effect.
Row 1: K1, * YO, K2 tog *
Row 2 and all WS rows: P
Row 3: * K2 tog, YO * end
   with K1
Rep rows 1 - 4

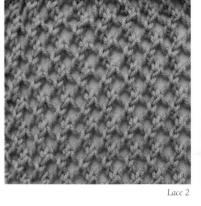

Lace 2

| K on RS, P on WS | P on RS, K on WS | T3B | T3F | C4B | Yarn Over | K2tog on RS, P2 tog on WS |

Lace 3

mult: an uneven number of stitches

Laces 3 and 4 are flat laces consisting of holes made on a stockinette stitch background. Flat laces are easy to design on graph paper. Each hole is created by a yarn-over. On the graph paper, place the YO's (an increase), where you want them, then add a K2tog (a decrease) for each YO.

Row 1: K
Row 2 and all WS rows: P
Row 3: K1, * YO, K2 tog *
Rep rows 1 - 4

Lace 3

Lace 4

C.o. 22 stitches

This lace was designed as a panel to be used amongst other stitch patterns. Follow the graph.

Lace 4

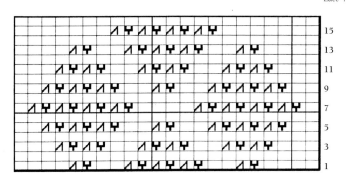

Lace 5

mult of 4, beginning with at least 8 sts

Doubling up on the YO's makes larger holes in the fabric.

Row 1: (WS) * K2tog, (YO) twice, K2 tog, *
Row 2: (RS) * K1, (K1, P1) into double YO, K1 *
Row 3: K2, * K2 tog, (YO) twice, K2 tog, * end with K2
Row 4: K2, * K1 (K1, P1) into double YO, K1, * end with K2

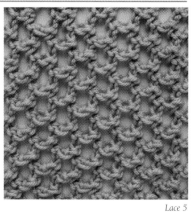

Lace 5

Lace 6

mult of 12 + 1

This lace demonstrates how the knitted fabric itself can be shaped by the use of YO's and K2tog's. Note the scalloped edges at top and bottom. This pattern is based on the "Old Shale" pattern commonly used for shawls or afghans.

Row 1: * K1, (K2tog) twice, (YO, K1) three times, K1, (K2tog) twice, * end with K1
Rows 2 and 3: K
Row 4: P

Lace 6

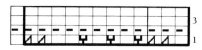

Lace 7

mult of 6
Row 1: * K1, YO, K2tog tbl, P1, K2tog, YO *
Row 2: P

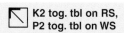

Lace 7

| K on RS, P on WS | — P on RS, K on WS | Yarn Over | K2tog on RS, P2 tog on WS | ssk | K2 tog. tbl on RS, P2 tog. tbl on WS |

Laces 8 through 10 incorporate decreases that accentuate the YO's. Different decreases have different effects:

K2tog—leans to the right, and is more pronounced if used before the YO (K2tog, YO)

ssk—leans to the left, and is more pronounced if used after the YO (YO, ssk)

SKpsso—leans to the left, and is more pronounced if used after a YO (SKpsso, YO)

K2tog tbl—leans to the left

Lace 8

mult of 7
Row 1: * K1, YO, K2 tog, K4 *
Row 2 and all WS rows: P.
Row 3: * K2, YO, K2 tog, K3 *
Row 5: * K3, YO, K2 tog, K2 *
Row 7: * K4, YO, K2 tog, K1 *
Row 9: * K3, K2tog tbl, YO, K2 *
Row 11: * K2, K2 tog tbl, YO, K3 *
Row 13: * K1, K2 tog tbl, YO, K4 *
Row 15: * K2 tog tbl, YO, K5 *
Rep rows 1 - 16

Lace 8

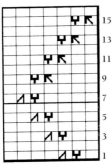

Lace 9

mult of 9 sts
Row 1: * K1, YO, K2 tog tbl, K3, K2 tog, YO, K1 *
Row 2 and all WS rows: P.
Row 3: * K2, YO, K2 tog tbl, K1, K2 tog, YO, K2 *
Row 5: * K3, YO, Sl 1, K2 tog, psso, YO, K3 *
Row 7: K
Rep rows 1 -8

Lace 9

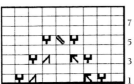

Lace 10

mult of 12
Note how the YO and decreases change places from the lower to the upper part of the diamond shape. This was done to retain the outlining. Decorative bobbles are added to this lace pattern.
Row 1: *P1, YO, ssk, K5, K2tog, YO, P1, K1 *
Row 2 and all WS rows: P.
Row 3: * P1, K1, YO, ssk, K3, K2tog, YO, K1, P1, K1 *
Row 5: * P1, K2, YO, ssk, K1, K2tog, YO, K2, P1, K1 *
Row 7: *P1, K4, B, K4, P1, K1 *
Row 9: * P1, K2, K2tog, YO, K1, YO, ssk, K2, P1, K1 *
Row 11: * P1, K1, K2tog, YO, K3, YO, ssk, K1, P1, K1 *
Row 13: * P1, K2tog, YO, K5, YO, ssk, P1, K1 *
Row 15: same as row 7
Rep rows 1 - 16

Lace 10

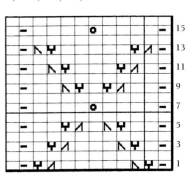

| ☐ K on RS, P on WS | ⊟ P on RS, K on WS | ⊔ Yarn Over | ◸ K2tog on RS, P2 tog on WS | ◹ K2 tog. tbl on RS, P2 tog. tbl on WS | ◩ ssk | ◯ Bobble |

Lace 11

This is an example of creating an original design using the principles given so far. To knit this pattern, follow the graph. Then, devise a design of your own.

Lace 11

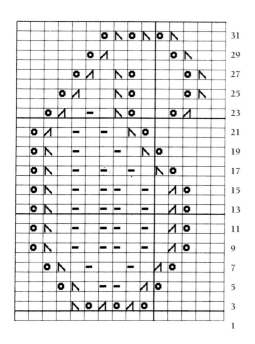

Laces 13 through 15 are yet more intricate than those above. In these patterns, stitches are placed in ways that "pull" the lines of the stockinette stitch into diagonal directions. This type of lace takes a great deal of ingenuity to design because it is necessary to think sculpturally. The rows may not have the same number of stitches because a YO may occur in one row, and a corresponding decrease may happen a row or more later. Note how in Lace 13 the increases work to make each "leaf" dimensional.

Lace 13

mult of 9
Row 1: * P2, K1, YO, K3tog, YO, K1, P2 *
Row 2 and all WS rows: K the P sts, and P all remaining sts
Row 3: * P2, K1, YO, K3, YO, K1, P2 *
Row 5: * P2, K1, YO, K5, YO, K1, P2 *
Row 7: * P2, K1, YO, K2tog tbl, K3tog, K2 tog, YO, K1, P2 *
Row 9: * P2, K1, K2tog tbl, K1, K2tog, K1, P2 *
Rep rows 1 - 10

Lace 13

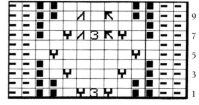

Lace 12

mult of 8

Cables are added to a lace pattern.
Row 1: * K2tog, YO, K4, YO, ssk *
Row 2 and all WS rows: P
Row 3: * K2tog, YO, C4B, YO, ssk *
Continue as established, working the cable on every sixth row.

Lace 12

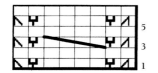

| ☐ K on RS, P on WS | — P on RS, K on WS | ╲ ssk | ⬭ Bobble | Ⴤ Yarn Over | ■ no stitch | ╱ K2tog on RS, P2 tog on WS | **3** K3tog. | ╲ K2 tog. tbl on RS, P2 tog. tbl on WS |

Lace 14

mult of 8 + 4

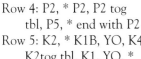

An old pattern called "Traveling Vine."

Row 1: K2, * YO, K1B, YO, K2tog tbl, K5, * end with K2

Row 2: P2, * P4, P2 tog tbl, P3, * end with P2

Row 3: K2, * YO, K1B, YO, K2, K2tog tbl, K3 * end with K2

Row 4: P2, * P2, P2 tog tbl, P5, * end with P2

Row 5: K2, * K1B, YO, K4, K2tog tbl, K1, YO, * end with K2.

Row 6: P2, * P1, P2tog tbl, P6, * end with P2

Row 7: K2, * K5, K2tog, YO, K1B, YO, * end with K2

Row 8: P2, * P3, P2tog, P4, * end with P2

Row 9: K2, * K3, K2tog, K2, YO, K1B, YO, * end with K2

Row 10: P2, * P5, P2tog, P2, * end with P2

Row 11: K2, * YO, K1, K2tog, K4, YO, K1B, * end with K2

Row 12: P2, * P6, P2tog, P1, * end with P2

Lace 14

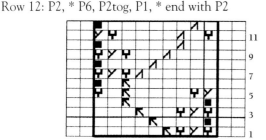

Lace 15

mult of 12 + 1

This is an adaptation of an old lace pattern. One way to learn about laces is to try to adapt an existing pattern.

Row 1, 21, and 23: * P1, K2tog, K3, YO, P1, YO, K3, K2tog tbl * end with P1

Row 2 and all WS rows: P

Row 3: * P1, K2tog, K2, YO, K1, P1, K1, YO, K2, K2tog tbl * end with P1

Row 5: * P1, K2tog, K1, YO, K2, P1, K2, YO, K1, K2tog tbl * end with P1

Row 7: * P1, K2tog, YO, K3, P1, K3, YO, K2tog tbl * end with P1

Rows 9, 11, and 13: * P1, YO, K3, K2tog tbl, P1, K2tog, K3, YO * end with P1

Row 15: * P1, K1, YO, K2, K2tog tbl, P1, K2tog, K2, YO, K1 * end with P1

Row 17: * P1, K2, YO, K1, K2tog tbl, P1, K2tog, K1, YO, K2 * end with P1

Row 19: * P1, K3, YO, K2tog tbl, P1, K2tog, YO, K3 * end with P1

Rep rows 1 - 24

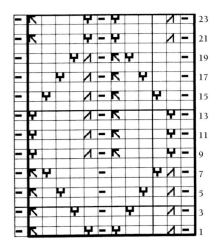

Lace 15

| | K on RS, P on WS | — | P on RS, K on WS | ■ | no stitch | Yarn Over | K2 tog. tbl on RS, P2 tog. tbl on WS | K2tog on RS, P2 tog on WS | K1B |

TEXTURES AND SPECIAL EFFECTS

Note the different textural effects created by twisting, dropping, increasing and decreasing, slipping, and wrapping stitches. Graphs are not given for these stitch patterns. You can graph them by choosing a symbol for each of the specialty stitches.

Slipped Stitches

mult of 2
Slipping a stitch on the RS row and working it on the WS creates an elongated stitch.
Row 1: * K1, sl 1 purlwise *
Row 2: P

Slipped Stitches

K or P into the back loop of each stitch.

Row 1: * K1B *
Row 2: * P1B *

K or P into the back loop of each stitch.

Dec on one row, inc on the next.

mult of 2
Row 1: * K2tog *
Row 2: * K into front and back of stitch *

Decrease on one row, increase on the next.

Triple Stitch

mult of 4
Row 1 and all RS rows: P
Row 2: * (K, P, K into next st), P3tog *
Row 4: * P3tog, (K, P, K into next st) *

Triple Stitch

Dropped Stitch

Drop a stitch off the needle and ravel it to the bottom of the knitting.

Dropped Stitch

Popcorn

Into the next stitch, (K into front of loop, K into back of loop) three times and slide st off needle. Then bring second, third, and fourth, fifth, and sixth sts over the first.

Popcorn

Wrapped Stitches

To wrap the next four sts, insert needle between fourth and fifth sts on left-hand needle from front to back, pick up yarn and pull through, then K2tog, K2.

Wrapped Stitches

Bobble

Into the next stitch, (K into front of loop, K into back of loop) three times and slide st off needle. [Turn the knitting and P the 6 sts. Turn, and K the sts]. Then bring second, third, and fourth, fifth, and sixth sts over the first. For a larger bobble, repeat the instructions in the parentheses.

Bobble

Right Twist

mult of 2

Row 1: from the front, knit through the back loop of the second stitch, then K the first st and slide both off the needle.

Row 2: P

Right Twist

Elongated Stitches

Wrap the yarn around the needle twice, and in the following row, drop off the two extra loops. The "block" effect in this swatch was done the same as the Bobble: turn the knitting and work stockinette stitch until three extra rows are created.

Elongated Stitches

CHAPTER 3

THE SHAPE
OF THINGS
TO COME

The most important defining characteristic of a sweater is its sleeve type. Sleeve types influence the shape of the entire sweater. For instance, the straight sleeve fits square with the sweater back and front pieces with no shaping done to the armhole area. The rounded form of the cap sleeve also takes a shaped armhole, and the raglan style is formed of a steady slope of sleeve and body pieces all the way up to the neckline. The dolman style presented in this book is made all-in-one with the sweater body (dolman sleeves can also be made separately).

Other, more secondary, characteristics include length of sweater body and sleeves, cardigan versus pullover, neckline treatment, cuffs or edgings, and other details that can be applied to a sweater of any of the sleeve styles. Let this chapter suggest some of the options in putting together a style that you may like to knit. Make sketches of your ideas.

SLEEVE STYLES

Straight Sleeve

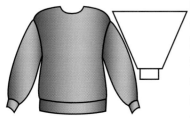

(See page 53 for the worksheet *Straight Sleeve Sweater*). The majority of the sweaters in this book are of the straight sleeve type, a style that is sometimes called "dropped shoulder." The sleeve top is bound off straight across with no armhole shaping done to the sweater body pieces. Because of its simple form, it is ideal for making elaborate stitch-patterned and color-worked sweaters, and also for beginning knitters.

Make the top of the sleeve wide enough for comfort. It should be a minimum of 6" (15cm) wider than the measurement of your upper arm. There is no maximum width, so go where your sense of style takes you!

If you like, the sleeve can be knitted directly onto the sweater front and back pieces thus eliminating a seam. See the "Pick Up and Knit Technique" on page 125.

The sleeve can be set-in slightly by knitting indents into the armhole area of the sweater front and back pieces, with a similar shaping to the upper sleeve. For examples, see **Autumn Tones** on page 122, and **Polar Bear** on page 128.

Cap Sleeve

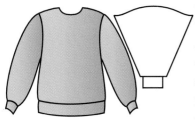

(See page 74 for the worksheet *Cap Sleeve Sweater*.) A cap sleeve consists of a rounded sleeve top that is fitted into a shaped armhole. If you stand sideways in front of a mirror, you can see the rounded shape of your upper arm where it attaches to your shoulder. The cap sleeve is designed to follow this shape. The armhole of the sweater is indented and slightly shaped, with a corresponding indent to the sleeve top.

The traditional fit for a cap sleeve is to have the seam at the very top of the arm where it meets the shoulder, with a small amount of ease in the upper sleeve. If the upper sleeve is close-fitted, the sleeve cap will also be narrowly shaped.

The sleeve also adapts well to the oversized look. If the upper sleeve is designed with plenty of ease, the top of the cap will fit lower on the upper arm, creating a "dropped shoulder" and the sleeve cap will be shaped wide.

A cap sleeve can also be knitted wider than the armhole and sewn in gathers to the armhole to make a puffy sleeve top, a style that fashionably emerges now and then.

Raglan Sleeve

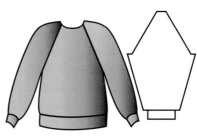

(See page 94 for the worksheet *Raglan Sleeve Sweater*.) The raglan sleeve style brings the top of the sleeve all the way to the neckline. After a slight initial bind-off, the upper sleeve incorporates steady shaping, as do the sweater's upper front and back pieces.

The row gauge (see Gauge Swatch on page 12) must be accurate; if it is off (even only slightly), the depth of the armhole will be too short, or longer than expected.

Using graph paper, it is easy determine the necessary shaping of both sweater body and sleeve pieces.

Decreases for Raglan and V-Neck Shaping

"Fully-fashioned" shaping places the decrease stitches in from the edge. The decrease stitches can be placed one, two, or three stitches in from the edge of the knitting.

To decrease:

• at the beginning of a RS (knit) row: K1, ssk, complete row.
• at the end of a RS row: knit up to last 3 stitches, K2 tog, K1.
• at the beginning of WS (purl) row: P1, P2 tog, completerow.
• at the end of WS row: work up to last 3 stitches, P2 tog tbl, P1.

Dolman Sleeves

Although dolman sleeves can be made separately, see the worksheet *One-Piece Dolman Sweater* on page 84, in which they are treated as one with the sweater.

Width of Upper Sleeves

It is important to fit this part of the sweater carefully, because this area has much to do with both the style and the comfort of the sweater. See the sweater, **Elegance in Cotton** on page 58 for the stylish effect of a wide upper sleeve. When you measure to fit the sweater, you will make this determination by checking various widths before a mirror.

Narrow sleeves are best in the cap or raglan styles due to the sleeve and armhole shaping that helps to reduce bulk in the underarm area.

I prefer generously-wide upper sleeves, both for freedom of movement and to avoid trapping heat. Any of the sleeve styles can accommodate as much width as you wish to add.

You will need to find your own upper arm comfort zone. One of the best ways to do this is to compare sweatshirts and sweaters in your wardrobe, and use the upper arm measurement of the garment that fits most comfortably. Also check with the Basic Dimensions chart in the Appendix.

Sleeve Increases

Sleeves begin narrow at the wrist and are increased up to the armhole (unless you have a different shape in mind). Here are some different ways the increases can be done:

a. Spread the increases evenly over the length of the sleeve.
b. Work the increases on every right-side row until the sleeve is the width desired, then knit the remainder of the sleeve straight up.
c. Work the increases so there are more at the beginning, and fewer at the upper parts of the sleeve, creating a greater slope at the beginning and less further along.
d. To make a "blousy" lower sleeve, work increases in the row above the cuff adding most or all of the stitches needed.

SWEATER BODY AND SLEEVE LENGTHS

There are four more or less standard sweater lengths for

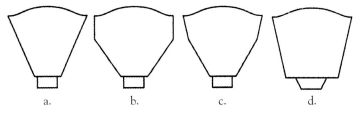

a.　　　b.　　　c.　　　d.

the body of the sweater. These include (from left to right in the illustration) waist, hip, crotch, and below crotch (tunic). These are traditional sweater lengths only, and you should feel free to also knit knee, mid-calf, above-waist, or any length you wish.

Long sleeves can be knitted to fit at the wrist, upper hand, or knuckles. Short sleeves can be made anywhere between the elbow and the upper arm. You can also make 3/4-length or 7/8-length sleeves that fit anywhere between the elbow and the wrist.

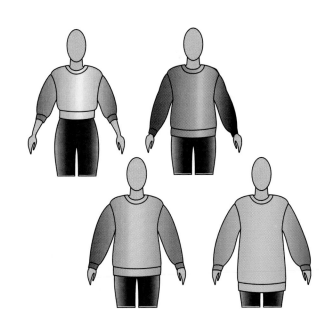

CUFFS OR EDGINGS

Ribbings are the most common way of finishing the edges of a sweater. Cuffs or edgings can be used to create a close fit such as a stretchy K/P ribbing worked in wool. Or, to merely stabilize the edges of the knitting and prevent curling and distortion, a non-elastic pattern stitch can be used. See pages 26 - 27 for some elastic and non-elastic ribbings.

Some additional ways to finish the edges of a sweater:

Knit a hem. Knit about 1" in stockinette stitch that is later turned to the inside and sewn in place.

Knit several rows in garter stitch, or any firm pattern stitch.

Make a curled edge by knitting in stockinette stitch for an inch or more.

Cuffs for the sleeves and bottom of the sweater can be any length you prefer—from a mere 1/2" to several inches. Sleeve cuffs can be made extra long with thumb holes, see page 78.

Tip:

If you are not sure how many stitches to use for the ribbing, knit it last by picking up stitches on the sweater body or sleeves. That way, if it isn't right, it can be ripped out and easily re-knitted.

Use needles that are at least two sizes smaller than those used to obtain the stitch gauge for the sweater to make a firmer stitch, and if desired, use fewer stitches for the edging to draw it in a little more.

A simple formula for how many stitches to use for the body ribbing is to use 90 percent of the sweater body stitches.

Using a calculator:
Number of sweater body stitches minus 10 percent
Round up or down to the nearest even number if knitting a 1 x 1 rib, or use your pattern stitch multiple. For the sleeves:
Number of stitches at lower sleeve minus 20 percent

NECKLINE STYLES

The basic neckline shapes are Boat, Round, V, and Square. These can be finished with ribbing or another suitable pattern stitch.

The back neck of the sweater is often knitted straight across but, if you like, it can be shaped similarly to the front but making it only about 1" (2.5cm) deep (except for the boat neck).

Boat Neck

The upper edge of the front and back parts of the sweater are knitted straight across, and the shoulders are sewn leaving an opening for the neck. The length of the shoulder seams is found by trying the sweater on.

To obtain a firm edge, use needles about two sizes smaller than those used for the sweater for the final 1" of sweater front and back pieces. A ribbing stitch can be used, or garter stitch, or any stitch that prevents curling. To make a hemmed boat neck, knit in stockinette stitch for an extra 1" (2.5cm); turn this amount to the inside and sew loosely in place. Then,

when sewing the shoulders, sew into the fold of the hem (see **Cotton Tunic** on page 60). See **Elegance in Cotton** on page 58 for a variation in which the boat neck edge is sewn into a slight curve.

Round

A versatile style, this neck shaping is used to make a crewneck, mock turtle, or a turtleneck. Other variations can include making a wide neck opening for an off-the-shoulder look, and making a cowl or draped turtleneck by enlarging the opening or by making the turtleneck wider and longer.

Take care that the opening will accommodate the size of your head if you are making a pullover. You can roughly calculate the size of an opening before knitting it by adding together the widths and depths of the neck opening and then comparing with the size of your head. The opening can usually be a little smaller than your head because knitting stretches.

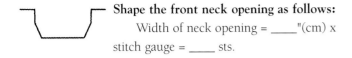

Shape the front neck opening as follows:
Width of neck opening = _____ "(cm) x stitch gauge = _____ sts.

If you are making a crewneck, allow for the width of the ribbing (if the ribbing will be 1" wide, add an extra 2" to the width of the neck opening).

Bind off approximately 4/5 of the stitches (or put them on a holder). Attach a second ball of yarn so that both sides of the neck can be worked at the same time. Decrease one stitch at each side of the neck opening until all decreases are made. Work even to the total length of the sweater.

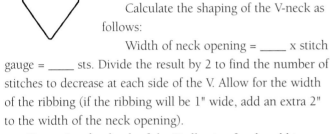

Square
Calculate the stitches the same as for the round neck, but bind off (or put on a holder) all stitches at once. Knit the sides of the neck straight up.

V-Shaped
Calculate the shaping of the V-neck as follows:
Width of neck opening = _____ x stitch gauge = _____ sts. Divide the result by 2 to find the number of stitches to decrease at each side of the V. Allow for the width of the ribbing (if the ribbing will be 1" wide, add an extra 2" to the width of the neck opening).

Determine the depth of the V, allowing for the ribbing:
Depth x row gauge = _____ rows.

This gives the number of rows over which the decreases are worked. Compare with the number of stitches to be decreased, and spread them equally along the edge of the V. The decreases can be arranged so that the upper 1" to 2" of the V is worked even to the top of the sweater. If you have difficulty figuring out how to distribute the decreases, plot them on graph paper, then use the graph as your knitting pattern.

To begin the shaping, first see that the sweater is an uneven number of stitches; if necessary CO one stitch at the beginning edge. Knit up to two stitches before the center stitch, work the first decrease, bind off the center stitch, and continue to shape the V, attaching a second ball of yarn to work both sides at once. See Decreases for V-Neck Shaping on page 41.

For a variation on the v-neck, see **Purple Tango** on page 68, for which the neckline shaping is made to accommodate a simple shawl collar.

Knitting the Neckband

To knit a neckband on two needles, first sew up one shoulder seam. If you are using a circular needle, sew both shoulder seams. Begin picking up stitches at one unsewn shoulder if using two needles, and at either shoulder if using a circular needle.

To figure out how many stitches to pick up, use a tape measure to carefully measure around the neck opening. Multiply by the sweater body stitch gauge, then subtract 5 percent to 10 percent of the stitches.

Neck opening = _____ x sweater stitch gauge = _____ - (minus) _____ percent = _____ sts.

More often than any other area of the sweater, the neckband may require adjustment after knitting. If you find after knitting it that it is either too loose or too snug, rip out and pick up a more appropriate number of stitches and re-knit the band. It should be comfortable to wear, and not distort the neck area of the sweater by either stretching or pulling on it.

Round Neckband

Using needles one to two sizes smaller than those for the sweater, pick up the stitches evenly along the entire edge. When you get to the bound-off stitches at the front neck, pick up one for each. Knit to the length desired, and then bind off loosely in the same pattern stitch. Sew the remaining shoulder and the neckband seam.

For a hemmed crewneck, knit twice the length desired, bind off loosely. Loosely sew the bound-off edge to the pick-up row.

V- and Square Neckbands

Using needles one-to-two sizes smaller than those for the sweater, pick up the stitches evenly along the entire edge. At the center front of the V-neck, pick up one where the stitch was bound off earlier. If needed, place a safety pin through it so it is easy to see.

At the center front of the V-neck and at the corners of the square neck, work shaping as follows. On right side rows, K2tog tbl, knit the center stitch, K2. On the wrong side, K2 tog, purl the center stitch, K2 tog tbl.

Front Openings

This topic is covered on page 117.

SHOULDER SEAM

The shoulder seam is important because it stabilizes the bound-off stitches of the upper front and back pieces. If you are tempted to knit the front and back pieces as one unit, keep in mind that the weight of the sweater can stretch the shoulder area out of shape.

If you like, the shoulders can be shaped. Stand before a mirror and determine the amount of slope your shoulder takes. Work two to four bind offs, making them the same for each shoulder, to approximate the shape of your shoulders. If you have relatively square shoulders, use only two bind-offs, or none at all.

QUICKIE SWEATERS

If you are new to sweater-knitting, you may be eager to see a finished product, and sometimes it is just plain fun to make a sweater that finishes quickly. Here are some suggestions for a design that will go more quickly than most:

- Use a plain pattern stitch such as stockinette, or reverse stockinette.
- Use "fat" yarn, a heavy worsted or bulky (keeping in mind that bulky yarns make warm sweaters, especially if they're wool).
- Have less to knit by choosing a smaller size, shorter body and sleeve lengths, large neck opening.
- Make a vest, a short sleeved, or sleeveless sweater.

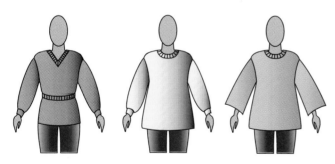

Ideas

Although the classic sweater style is knitted straight up to the armhole, there are other ways that sweaters can be shaped.

- As shown by the dolman style on page 83, fit a short sweater at the waist and increase up to the armhole.

- Decrease up to a fitted waist then increase up to the armhole.
- Flare the bottom of the sweater and decrease up to the armhole. Flare the sleeves also, or not.

SWEATERS IN TWO PIECES

The classic sweater set consists of a sleeveless fitted top worn under a buttoned cardigan.

The two-piece idea can also consist of a vest worn over a long-sleeve sweater (see **Trompe L'Oeil** on page 126 for an adaptation of this).

Figure Flattery

Here are a few hints on how best to enhance your figure.

For a slimming profile, choose an overall stitch pattern that creates a vertical "line" such as cables and wide ribbings, also use V-necks and front openings.

Thinner fabrics (fingering and sport weight yarns) are more slenderizing than heavier (worsted and bulky weights) ones.

Short, close-fitting styles tend to enhance a good figure or a person with short stature.

Bulky fabrics, horizontal stripes, and rounded necklines are wonderful on thin people.

Dropped shoulders, wide upper sleeves, hip- and tunic-lengths, bulky yarn weights, and large, dramatic stitch and color patterns are beneficial to tall people.

CHAPTER 4

FITTING THE SWEATER

F it is the backbone of garment design, and is the key to comfort, itself. Fit is also a very personal thing. A style that fits one person may be too big, too small, too short, or too long for the next. Personally, I like my sweaters to be roomy, and my winter ones to have extra-long sleeve cuffs and high turtlenecks. I think the reason for this is that my creative work makes me want to be free and unrestricted, and I know what keeps me warm. Our individual preferences regarding fit are important.

For this chapter you will need a tape measure, a mirror (full-length is best), a pencil, and paper.

Try to understand what type of fit you like and why. How do you like your clothes to make you feel? Do you prefer a "second skin," or would you rather be enveloped in sensuous drape? Do you like the reassurance of a garment's weight, or do you prefer to feel you are wearing nothing at all?

Try sketching a sweater that fulfills your idea of what a good "fit" means. What type of yarn will you use? Pattern stitch? Color?

For the worksheets for the *Straight, Cap, Dolman,* and *Raglan Sleeve Sweaters (see pages 52, 74, 84, 94)*, actual body measurements are used to determine the size of the sweater to be knitted. In other words, in one step you will be measuring yourself while also planning the size and shape of the sweater. The resulting dimensions are then easily translated into the number of stitches or rows to knit.

Do the *Measuring for Fit* worksheet on the facing page (see also page 138) for each sweater you knit, unless you are going to make each sweater exactly the same. If you are knitting a sweater for someone else, take his or her measurements, use the Standard Dimensions chart in the Appendix, or use the dimensions of an existing garment (sweater or sweatshirt).

Using a tape measure, stand before a mirror to be sure you are measuring correctly. Wear lightweight clothing for accuracy. After measuring, you may like to compare the measurements taken with those of a sweater that fits really well.

For convenience and extra copy of the Measuring for Fit Worksheet appears in the appendix

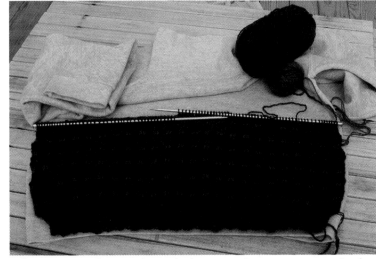

One way to fit a sweater is to knit according to the dimensions of an existing garment that fits comfortably.

EASE

Ease is the extra space inside the body and sleeves of a sweater. Ease is added so the garment can be put on and taken off easily, to provide the comfort of roominess, and for style. A sweater worn alone can be made more snug than one worn over another garment, and a pullover must have sufficient ease for getting in and out of. Plentiful ease can be more appropriate for sweaters made of finer yarns, with less ease needed with heavier yarns. "Stretchability" can take the place of ease. You will need to determine your own ease requirements for what makes you feel comfortable and is best for your appearance. My advice is to experiment with ease—use a little more or a little less with each sweater you knit.

Guidelines for amount of ease to allow in the body of the sweater:

Tightly-fitted	allow	0"
Close-fitting	allow	2"
Loose-fitting	allow	4"-6"
Oversized	allow	8"-10" or more

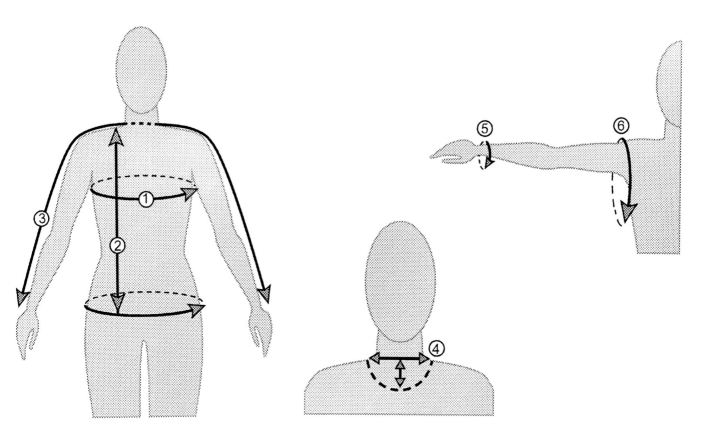

MEASURING FOR FIT WORKSHEET

1.) Measure around the widest part of your chest/bust area. Add ease to this measurement, according to the chart on page 46; also, check how the bottom of the sweater will fit, and make any necessary adjustments. The result is then divided in half for the front and back pieces of the sweater.

Chest/bust measurement = _____"(cm)
Add ease of ___"(cm) for a total of _____"(cm)
Total divided by 2 = _____"(cm) ①

2.) Measure from top of shoulder (the highest point along a normal shoulder seam), to exactly where you want the sweater to end. Do this standing before a mirror with the tape measure draped from your shoulder.

Shoulder to bottom of sweater = _____ "(cm) ②

3.) Measure from sleeve end to sleeve end. It is best to do this with arms at sides. It may be easier to measure from the nape of your neck to one sleeve end, and then multiply by two.

Sleeve end to sleeve end = _____"(cm) ③

4.) For the neck opening, measure the distance from the shoulder seam down to where the collar will end. For v or lower necklines, this is where you want the lowest point of the v (not including the ribbing). Measure to obtain the width of the neck opening. Because it is difficult to obtain these accurately, you may want to refer to the Standard Dimensions chart on page 142, or compare your results with an existing sweater.

Depth of neck opening = _____"(cm) ④
Width of neck opening = _____"(cm) ④

5.) Measure and add the amount of ease desired for the part of the sleeve just above the cuff. Loop the tape measure around your arm or wrist to find a comfortable circumference.

Width of lower sleeve = _____"(cm) ⑤

6.) Determine the fullness of the widest part of the sleeve by draping the tape measure around your upper arm. Allow ease. (See Information on Sleeves on page 40. One-half of ⑥ will be the depth of the armhole of the sweater.)

Width of upper sleeve = _____"(cm) ⑥

SPECIAL FITTING NEEDS

- *Pregnancy.* I personally balk at the idea of making a maternity sweater that is worn for several months and then put aside. Instead, make an oversized sweater that can be worn afterwards when you have those days where you feel like wrapping yourself in something big and cozy. Or, make a sweater for someone bigger than you, wear it while you need it, then hand it on.

- *Large hips and narrow chest.* To make a sweater that is hip-length or longer, measure around your hips and add ease. Measure your chest/bust and add ease. Multiply each by the stitch gauge, then subtract to find the number of stitches to be decreased from the bottom of the sweater to the armhole area. Divide by 2 to find the number of decrease rows—decreasing one stitch each end of a row. Decrease evenly between bottom and armhole of the sweater front and back.

- *Narrow hips and large chest.* These adjustments are the same as for large hips and narrow chest, but calculate the increases needed, instead of decreases.

Tips

You can work on the design of a sweater as you are knitting it. For an example of how this works, read through the instructions for the sweater, *Damask Block* on page 54.

Keep notes on each sweater you knit. Some designs you will likely use again, and others you may want to make with variations. I keep my notes in a small spiral notebook that stays in my knitting basket. For each sweater design I sketch a diagram of the pieces to be knitted, note dimensions, write out stitch patterns, and include a yarn description, needle sizes, gauge, and numbers of stitches to be knitted.

When following a purchased sweater pattern, compare the dimensions of the design to those you've determined using your measurements and desired amount of ease. This will give an indication of how the garment will fit.

Keep a notebook to jot down the particulars of each sweater you knit, and to sketch out ideas for future projects.

CHECKING FIT AS YOU KNIT

Although measurements provide crucial information for achieving an accurate fit, it is still a good idea to check the fit as you proceed. Here is how to do this for the individual sweater pieces.

Back/Front

Knit halfway across a row, spread the knitting out along both needles, then hold the piece up to yourself while standing before a mirror. Check that width and length will be as intended.

Sleeves

Spread the stitches out along both needles and drape the piece over your outstretched arm. Check length and width, and the fit of the cuff.

Neckline

After you've begun the neckline ribbing, check that you have the appropriate number of stitches by slipping the stitches onto a long, circular needle. Try on the sweater. If knitting a turtleneck, try on to check the length of the neck ribbing.

CHAPTER 5

SOME
SWEATERS
TO KNIT

This section includes worksheets for making four sweater styles: Straight Sleeve, Cap Sleeve, Dolman, and Raglan. Find a style that you will be comfortable knitting and wearing, or experiment with all of them. Sweater designs are given as examples—refer to them for ideas and for specific knitting instructions. If you are not yet comfortable with designing a sweater on your own, several sizes are given for most of the sweaters. For any of them, try adapting lengths and widths to suit your own fitting needs. Further on in the chapter are additional ideas to work with—how to plan for a front opening, designing a sweater in sections, and other creative ideas. Begin anywhere you like, but do try something that challenges your creative impulses.

Note also the blended yarns used for the sweaters in this chapter. In **Damask Block**, two similar wool yarns blend their colors. In **Elegance in Cotton, Cotton Tunic,** and **Cotton Cover-Up,** two soft and slightly textured cottons were plied for interesting colorings in a soft, drapey fabric. **Fuchsia Takes a Ribbing** consists of wool blended with cotton to make a fabric that blends the qualities of both. **Purple Tango** is comprised of two cottons and a chenille to result in a luxuriously textured, velvety soft fabric. Experiment with combinations of your own to create a unique yarn.

Note: Yardages are given for some of the sweaters, and these are to be considered approximate only. It is best that you make a yardage swatch of your yarn, and compare it with the dimensions of the sweater that you wish to knit (see "Estimating Yardage" on page 12). Where yardages are not given, it is assumed that you are using leftover yarns, or that you will be changing the design to suit your own ideas.

DESIGNING A STRAIGHT-SLEEVE SWEATER

To knit a sweater using this worksheet, first do *Measuring for Fit* (page 47) to determine sweater sleeve and body lengths and widths, and neckline shaping (neck shaping is optional—see **Damask Block** on page 54, and **Elegance in Cotton** on page 58).

The diagram shows the four main pieces of the sweater, and how they fit together. (The sweater back is shown upside down—it is actually knitted from the bottom up.) The numbers from *Measuring for Fit* (page 47) correspond to the diagram with ① resulting in the number of stitches to knit for front and back pieces of the sweater. ② is the length to knit the sweater, and so on.

Follow the directions accompanying the worksheet to knit a sweater.

STRAIGHT SLEEVE SWEATER WORKSHEET

Procedure:
    Do the worksheet Measuring for Fit (page 47)
    Choose a yarn and find gauges
Stitch gauge = ____
Row gauge = ____

① x stitch gauge = ____ stitches to knit for each of back and front.
Subtract 10 percent = ____ stitches for ribbing.. . . . ./

② = ____ "(cm): length to knit for each of front and back. . . ⟶

② minus ④ (depth) = ____ "(cm): begin neck bind offs. . .

④ (width) x stitch gauge = ____ stitches to bind off for neck.

⑤ x stitch gauge = ____ stitches for beginning of sleeve above ribbing. . . . .

Subtract 20 percent = ___ stitches for ribbing.
— · — · — · — · — · — · — · — · — · — · —

③ minus ① = ____ "(cm).
Divide the result by 2 = ____ "(cm): Length of sleeve.

⑥ x stitch gauge = ____ stitches at top of sleeve.

⑤ x stitch gauge = ____ stitches above ribbing.
Subtract to =   ____ stitches to be increased. Divide by
        2 = ____ | total increase rows. |

Subtract length of ribbing from sleeve length = ____ "(cm)
x row gauge = ____ total rows.

    Divide by 2 = ____ | total RS rows. |

Instructions

Needle size for body of sweater ____
Needle size for ribbing ____

Back

Cast on this number of stitches using the smaller needle size. Work desired length of ribbing. Change to larger needles, increase to the number of stitches to knit for the back.

Knit the back to this length and bind off.

Front

Knit the front same as the back up to here. Shape the neckline according to the instructions for your preferred neck style (page 42). Work to same length as back and bind off all stitches.

Sleeves

Cast on this number of stitches using the smaller needle size. Work desired length of ribbing. Change to larger needles, and increase to the number of stitches to knit for the sleeve.

Compare the increase rows with the total RS rows, and distribute increases evenly on RS rows to top of sleeve, or see sleeve-increase methods on page 41. Bind off all stitches. Make second sleeve the same. See page 43 for finishing the neck. Sew the pieces of the sweater together.

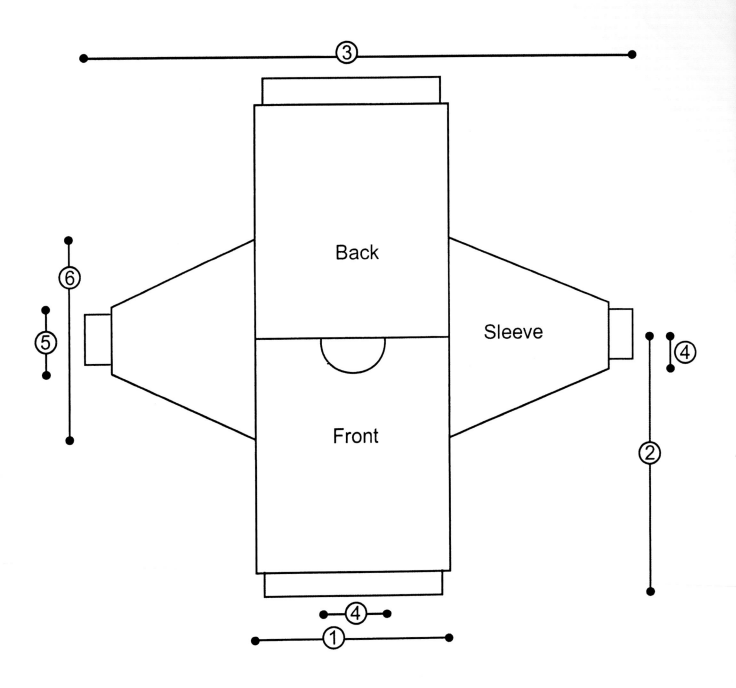

DAMASK
BLOCK

Read through the following instructions or, better yet, *knit* this sweater! This easy-to-knit sweater is presented in a way that is different from other sweaters in this book. The idea is to help you understand the process involved in designing a sweater, how decisions are made, and how the sweater comes together. At each point where I made a decision, you may make one of your own, varying the design to suit your own ideas or needs. The instructions refer to the worksheet *Measuring for Fit* on page 47, and the worksheet for *Straight Sleeve Sweaters* on page 52.

Sizes

Directions are for size Medium with a finished circumference of 44"/112cm. (Sizes Small 40"/101.5cm, and Large 48"/122cm, are in parentheses.)

Yarn

For an easy sweater, a worsted weight yarn also makes a quicker project than a lightweight yarn, so, from my stash of wool yarns I decided to ply two sport weights by holding them together as I knitted. (You can use a single strand of worsted weight yarn instead, if you wish.) I tried different color combinations and knitted several color swatches, and discovered that purple with rust met with my liking. The yarns are a smooth texture, so a pattern stitch will show up well.

Yardage

1580 (1420, 1750) yards of each color.

Needles

Size 8 needles are appropriate for the yarn (I also tried 7's and 9's), with size 6 needles for the edgings.

Pattern Stitch

It was my objective to design an easy-to-knit sweater, but one that also had an interesting pattern stitch. I decided on a combination of stockinette and garter stitch, using plain garter for the cuffs. After knitting a number of swatches and thinking about what combination would make an interesting pattern stitch, the idea of making garter stitch "blocks" arrived.

Garter Block Pattern Stitch

(Cast on a multiple of 10 sts.
Note: the garter stitch is worked by purling on every row.)
Row 1: * K5, P5 *
Row 2: Purl
Rep these two rows for a total of eight rows (the garter stitch sections will have four ridges)
Row 9: * P5, K5 *
Row 10: Purl
Repeat these two rows for a total of eight rows. Repeat rows 1–16 for pattern.

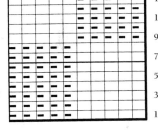

Swatch and Gauge

To be sure of the combination of pattern stitch and yarn choice, and to establish the gauge, I knit a swatch of the pattern stitch. Wanting the swatch to be at least 4" square, I used 20 sts, or 2 multiples of the stitch pattern, and knit for about 4".

Gauge on size 8 needles
4 sts and 6 rows = 1"/2.5cm.

☐ K on RS, P on WS   — P on RS, K on WS

Here are a couple of pattern stitch variations on this sweater that you may like to consider.

Variation 1. Make the cuffs in garter stitch as the sweater shown here, and the body and sleeves in stockinette stitch. This eliminates the pattern stitch, but retains the basic style of the sweater.

Variation 2. Work the garter and stockinette sections in stripes instead of blocks. (Repeat rows 1 and 2 of the pattern stitch throughout.)

Look for ways to vary stitch pattern ideas and try to visualize how the finished sweater will look in them.

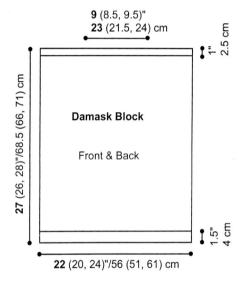

9 (8.5, 9.5)"
23 (21.5, 24) cm

1"
2.5 cm

Damask Block

Front & Back

27 (26, 28)"/68.5 (66, 71) cm

1.5"
4 cm

22 (20, 24)"/56 (51, 61) cm

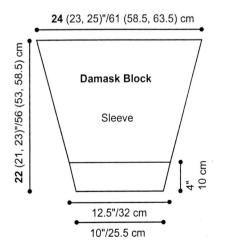

24 (23, 25)"/61 (58.5, 63.5) cm

Damask Block

Sleeve

22 (21, 23)"/56 (53, 58.5) cm

4"
10 cm

12.5"/32 cm

10"/25.5 cm

To begin knitting, all I need is to find the width of front and back pieces. I will think about the neck treatment and the sleeve styles as I knit.

Beginning with ① of *Measuring for Fit* (page 47), I determine the width of the sweater. A 44"/112cm circumference gives me about 10"/25.5cm of ease, about what I like. 44"/112cm divided by two gives a 22"/56cm width for each of the back and front pieces. And now we apply the gauge to the width: 22"/56cm x 4 sts per inch/2.5cm = 88, and this is rounded to the nearest multiple of 10 (necessary because the pattern stitch requires a multiple of 10) to equal 90 stitches.

I then decide on the length of the sweater (② of *Measuring for Fit*). I would like this sweater long for casual wear, and go for a total length of 27 (26, 28)"/68.5 (66, 71)cm.

In my notebook, I begin to sketch a diagram showing the general shape of the sweater, filling in the dimensions and numbers of stitches used. I make sure to write down the pattern stitch, the gauge, and needle size information.

Begin to Knit

Now we can begin to knit the back piece of the sweater. For the bottom edge of the sweater, I used needles two sizes smaller than for the remainder of the sweater. So, on size 6 needles, I cast on 90 (80, 100) stitches. Knitting in garter stitch I stop at 1-1/4"/3cm, which appears to be a suitable length for the edging. Changing to size 8 needles, I proceed to knit the back of the sweater beginning with row 1 of the Garter Block pattern stitch.

Planning the Neckline

While knitting, I'm thinking about the neck treatment. A garter stitch boat neck will work well, because it will match the garter stitch edging at the bottom of the sweater. So I plan to end the pattern stitch 1"/2.5cm short of the top of the sweater, and then to work in garter stitch using size 6 needles for 1"/2.5cm. I finish the back of the sweater this way, also noting the boat neck decision in my notebook.

The front of the sweater is knitted exactly the same as the back, because the neckline is the same on both front and back. (For a different type of neckline, I would calculate where to stop in order to begin the neckline shaping.)

Planning the Sleeves

While knitting, I think about the sleeves, and find I am torn between two ideas. I could make 3/4 length sleeves with a 1-1/4"/3cm garter stitch edging at the bottom edge. Or, I could make a fold-back garter stitch cuff (about 4"/10cm total length) on a full-length sleeve. I like both ideas, but since I need to choose one, I go for the full-length sleeve.

Using ⑤ and ⑥ of *Measuring for Fit*, I choose 10"/25.5cm for a lower sleeve circumference to make a loose-fitting cuff. Liking roomy upper sleeves, I drape the tape measure and decide on 24"/61cm for the sleeve top.

Using ③ of *Measuring for Fit*, I subtracted the 22"/56cm width of my sweater and determined that each sleeve will be 22 (21, 23)"/53 (51, 58.5)cm long. Of this, the cuff will take 2"/5cm (it is a 4"/10cm fold-back cuff), leaving 18 (17, 19)"/46 (43, 48)cm that will be knitted in pattern stitch with increases. With this information, I begin one sleeve.

I cast on to size 6 needles 40 stitches and knit in garter stitch (knit every row) for a total of 4"/10cm. Then I increase 10 sts (for a total of 50) as additional assurance that the cuff will fit more closely than the lower sleeve. This is done on the WS, so the pattern stitch can begin on the RS on the following row.

It is now necessary to calculate the sleeve increases. The sleeve begins with 50 sts and will end at 24 (23, 25)"/61 (58.5, 63.5)cm wide with 96 (92, 100) sts. 96 – 50 = 46 total increases, divided by two = 23 increase rows (since two stitches are increased per row).

The sleeve will be 18"/46cm long from above the cuff. 18" x 6 rows to the inch = 108 rows, divided by two = 54 RS rows. Comparing 23 inc rows with 54 RS rows tells me that the sleeve can be increased evenly almost to the top by working two increases on every other RS row (23 x 2 = 46), with a few rows left over. Therefore, increases will be

made every fourth row (every other RS row) until there are 96 (92, 100) sts, then the sleeve is worked straight to a total of 22 (21, 23)"/56 (53, 58.5)cm.

After one sleeve is knitted, I sew up the shoulder seams of the front and back pieces, then sew on the sleeve. I check the fit of the sleeve, and the length of the sweater. If there are any changes to be made, I take out the seams and make them, then knit the second sleeve.

Finishing

All parts for this sweater are finished and can be sewn together. Sew the shoulder seams, trying on the sweater to find the right size for the neck opening. The sleeves are sewn on next. Then sew the sleeve seams, and finally the side seams.

I check that the sleeve information and any changes are jotted into my notebook. If you knitted along, you now have a finished sweater and a completed pattern. If you think about this, it is done in a different order than the way you may have been taught—to buy a pattern, find a matching yarn, and to knit the sweater. Here, we have found a yarn, and then knitted the sweater and drafted the pattern at the same time.

THREE COTTON SWEATERS

The following three sweaters were machine knitted. Each is made of two fine, lightly slubbed cotton yarns that were plied into one strand on a spinning wheel. The designs can be hand knitted to the dimensions given, or, to achieve your own fit, use the worksheet, *Measuring for Fit* (page 47) and the worksheet *Straight Sleeve Sweater* (page 52). See instructions for the individual sweaters.

Yarn

Use the yarn of your choice (suggestions are given with each sweater), and find the yardage needed as per instructions on page 12.

Needles and Gauge

See page 12 to find the correct needle size, and to establish the gauge. You will also need to have needles that are two sizes smaller for knitting the hems.

Pattern Stitch

Choose a plain stitch such as stockinette for a textured yarn, or a pattern stitch for a plain yarn.

ELEGANCE
IN COTTON

Drape is important to this elegant and yet simply shaped sweater. Draped garments fall gracefully along the lines of the figure, and move with the motions of the wearer. There are certain additional features that bring this sweater out of the realm of the ordinary. The lower sleeve is made with an ease of only 3/4"/2cm so that the sleeve can be pulled up on the forearm and remain in place. The wide upper sleeve gives the sweater a graceful, elegant look. A softly curved neckline, created by turning the upper edge to the inside and hemming it, and using hems instead of ribbings give it a "couture" rather than a "sweater" look. To hand knit this sweater, choose a drapey fiber such as a soft cotton, silk, rayon yarn, or knitting ribbon.

Sizes

Small (Medium, Large), with finished circumferences of 42 (46, 50)"/106 (117, 127)cm.

Back and Front

C.o. using needles two sizes smaller than those used to obtain the gauge. Knit for 2"/5cm (1"/2.5cm of this will be hemmed to the back later). Change to the larger needles. Knit to the top and b.o. all sts. Knit the front the same.

Sleeves

C.o. with the smaller needles and knit for 2"/5cm (1"/2.5cm of this will be turned to the back later). Change to the larger needles and increase evenly to the top of the sleeve, then b.o. all sts.

Finishing

Sew the shoulders. Sew the sleeves on. Sew side and underarm seams. Turn in hems of sleeves, front and back 1"/2.5cm and sew loosely. To form a curved neckline, turn in the upper edge about 2"/5cm in the center tapering to almost nothing at the shoulder seams. Turn in the back neckline a small amount. Sew these loosely.

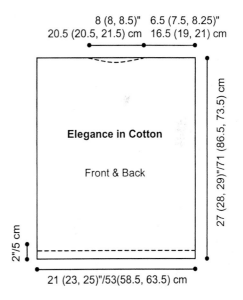

8 (8, 8.5)" 6.5 (7.5, 8.25)"
20.5 (20.5, 21.5) cm 16.5 (19, 21) cm

Elegance in Cotton

Front & Back

27 (28, 29)"/71 (86.5, 73.5) cm

2"/5 cm

21 (23, 25)"/53(58.5, 63.5) cm

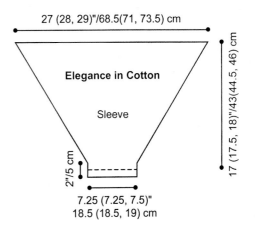

27 (28, 29)"/68.5(71, 73.5) cm

Elegance in Cotton

Sleeve

17 (17.5, 18)"/43(44.5, 46) cm

2"/5 cm

7.25 (7.25, 7.5)"
18.5 (18.5, 19) cm

Hems are a durable edge-finish.

COTTON
TUNIC

This tunic-length boat neck sweater is fashioned with wide sleeves that can be worn folded up if desired. The simple style, like **Elegance in Cotton** (page 58), can be knitted of a plain cotton, or a wool yarn for a casual look, or a silk or rayon yarn for a dressier appearance.

Sizes

Small (Medium, Large), with finished circumferences of 40 (44, 48)"/101.5 (112, 122)cm.

Back and Front

C.o. using needles two sizes smaller than those used to obtain the gauge. Knit for 2"/5cm (1"/2.5cm of this will be turned to the back later). Change to larger needles and knit up to 1"/2.5cm of the desired length of the sweater. Change to the smaller needles and knit for 2"/5cm. Make the front the same.

Sleeves

C.o. using the smaller needles, knit for 2"/5cm (1"/2.5cm of this will be turned to the back later). Change to the larger needles and increase evenly to the top of the sleeve. B.o. all sts.

Finishing

Hem the upper edges of front and back pieces by turning 1"/2.5cm to the back and stitching in place. Sew the shoulders at the fold of the hem, allowing sufficient neck opening to get the sweater on and off. Sew the sleeves on. Sew side and underarm seams. Turn in hems of sleeves and sweater body 1"/2.5cm and sew loosely.

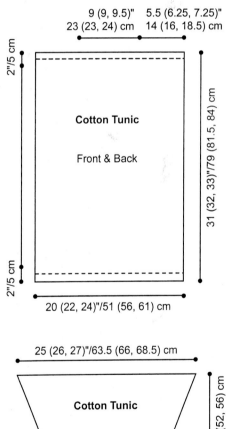

9 (9, 9.5)"   5.5 (6.25, 7.25)"
23 (23, 24) cm   14 (16, 18.5) cm

2"/5 cm

2"/5 cm

Cotton Tunic

Front & Back

31 (32, 33)"/79 (81.5, 84) cm

20 (22, 24)"/51 (56, 61) cm

25 (26, 27)"/63.5 (66, 68.5) cm

Cotton Tunic

Sleeve

20 (20.5, 22)"/51 (52, 56) cm

2"/5 cm

10.5 (11, 11.5)"
26 (27, 29) cm

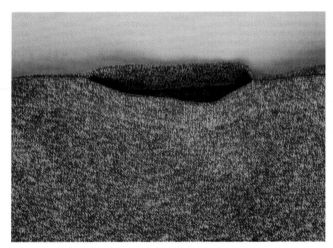

The boat neck is a simple way to make a neck opening.

COTTON
COVER-UP

A stand-up collar and roomy sleeves give distinction to this casual zip-front sweater that can be tossed on over a bathing suit or a t-shirt and jeans. Make it in cotton for cool, comfortable summer wear.

A zip-front sweater is easy to design because there is no front band to plan for. Begin with a 30"/76cm separating zipper, and plan the length of the front of the sweater including the collar, to match the zipper length.

The sleeve used for the sweater shown is the same as that for **Elegance in Cotton** (page 58). You can instead use the **Cotton Tunic** (page 60) sleeve if you prefer. Refer to the diagram to see how the parts of the sweater are fitted together.

Sizes

Small (Medium, Large), with finished circumferences of 40 (44, 48)"/101.5 (112, 122)cm.

Knit the back and sleeves the same as for **Cotton Elegance** (page 58). Knit each front 1/2 the width of the back, shaping the neck edges. See neckline shaping for a round neck on page 42. Sew the shoulder seams.

Collar

Measure the neck opening. Multiply by the stitch gauge. Cast on and knit 4"/10cm. Sew one long edge to the neck opening.

Zipper

Lay the sweater out flat. Baste the zipper to the fronts using sewing thread and placing the zipper 2"/5cm above the neck seam. Fold the collar in half lengthwise and secure it with pins. Enclose the zipper tapes into the open short ends of the collar and pin, then finish the tape ends by folding them to the back and stitching in place. Sew the long edge of the collar to the neck seam using yarn. Sew the zipper tapes in place using sewing thread. Thread a large needle with the sweater yarn and work a row of running stitch along each zipper tape through all layers.

Finishing

Sew the sleeves on. Sew sleeve and side seams. Sew hems of the body and sleeves.

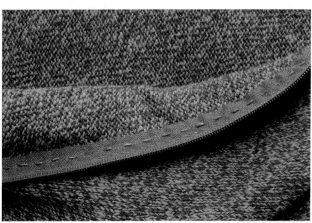

A running stitch is a decorative way to finish a zipper.

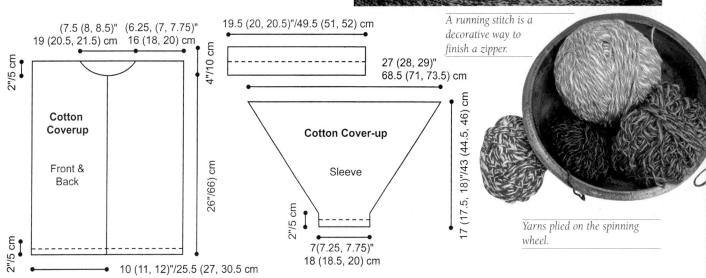

Yarns plied on the spinning wheel.

FUCHSIA
TAKES A
RIBBING

The interesting neck treatment of this sweater is its partially sewn-up turtleneck.

Ribbed sweaters follow the lines of the body. If you want to make a sweater that fits closely without feeling tight, choose a ribbed pattern stitch.

Two gauges are used for a ribbed, stretchy pattern stitch. This allows a comparison of the knitting when it is both in a relaxed state, and slightly stretched, and gives a better idea of how the sweater will fit than if only one gauge were used.

The sweater is made of two yarns, a wool in fuchsia and a cotton in dark multi-shades, blended by knitting them together. Wool and cotton meld nicely—you can feel both the wool and the cotton in the blend. The cotton adds softness, and the wool contributes to the springiness of the ribbed pattern stitch. The yarns give the right weight for a spring or fall season sweater … not too warm, and yet warm enough.

Sizes

Small (Medium, Large), with finished circumferences of 36"/91.5cm unstretched—40"/101.5cm slightly stretched (40-45, 44-50)"/(101.5-112, 112-127)cm.

Yarn

One strand of sport weight yarn is held together with a strand of fine cotton machine knitting yarn throughout (see Instructions for Using Coned Yarns on page 12). To substitute one yarn for the two, choose a heavy sport weight, or a light worsted weight that gets the same gauge.

Yardage

1300 (1500, 1650) yards of each color.

Needles

Sizes 7 and 5.

Gauge

5 sts unstretched or 4 sts slightly stretched, and 6 rows = 1"/2.5cm over Wide Ribbing pat st using size 7 needles.

Wide Ribbing

(mult of 4 sts)

Row 1: K3, P1

Row 2: K1, P3

Rep rows 1 and 2 for pat

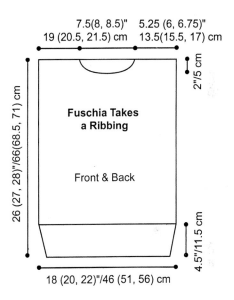

7.5(8, 8.5)"   5.25 (6, 6.75)"
19 (20.5, 21.5) cm   13.5(15.5, 17) cm

2"/5 cm

26 (27, 28)"/66(68.5, 71) cm

Fuschia Takes a Ribbing

Front & Back

4.5"/11.5 cm

18 (20, 22)"/46 (51, 56) cm

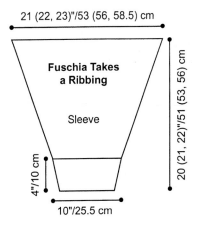

21 (22, 23)"/53 (56, 58.5) cm

Fuschia Takes a Ribbing

Sleeve

20 (21, 22)"/51 (53, 56) cm

4"/10 cm

10"/25.5 cm

☐ K on RS, P on WS	— P on RS, K on WS

Instructions

Back

With smaller needles, c.o. 80 (90, 100) sts. Work in 1 x 1 rib for 4 1/2"/11.5cm ending on a RS row. Next row (WS), P and inc 10 sts evenly spaced across row—90 (100, 110) sts. Change to larger needles and work in pat st until piece meas 26 (27, 28)"/66 (68.5, 71)cm from beg, then b.o. in ribbing.

Front

Work same as back. When piece measures 24 (25, 26)"/61 (63.5, 66)cm, shape neck: Work 30 (34, 38) sts, join a second ball of yarn and b.o. center 30 (32, 34) sts, work to end. Working both sides at once, b.o. 1 st at each neck edge every other row four times, until 26 (30, 34) sts rem at each shoulder. When piece meas same as back, b.o. all sts.

Sleeves

With smaller needles, c.o. 42 sts. Work in 1 x 1 rib for 4"/10cm ending on a RS row. Next row (WS), P and inc 18 sts evenly spaced across row—60 sts. Change to larger needles and work in pat st, inc one st each end every other row until 126 (130, 130) sts. When piece measures 20 (21, 22)"/51 (53, 56)cm from beg, b.o. all sts in ribbing.

Finishing

Sew right-hand shoulder seam. With smaller needles, pick up 94 (100, 106) sts evenly around neckline. Work in 1 x 1 rib for 9"/23cm. B.o. loosely in ribbing. Sew remaining shoulder seam. Starting at the base of the neck, sew up 4"/10cm of the turtleneck and fasten off securely. Sew on sleeves. Sew sleeve and side seams.

Blending cotton with wool creates a sweater fabric that has characteristics of both.

PURPLE
TANGO

This sweater is yummy to wear, and so luxuriously soft. Strands of three different yarns were held together throughout to create the yarn for this sweater, and not one of them is intended for hand knitting: a purple rayon chenille, a weaving yarn that knits into a fabric too flimsy to make a sweater even on very fine needles, and two fine, slubbed cottons made for machine knitting, one blue, and the other multi-colored. This combination knits to a bulky gauge, but the resulting fabric does not feel bulky, and has excellent drape.

The neckline treatment consists of a simple way to fashion a shawl collar. The collar is knitted directly onto the sloped edge of the neckline with its bottom edges overlapped and sewn in place.

Sizes

Small (Medium, Large), with finished circumferences of 38 (42, 46)"/96.5 (106, 117)cm.

Yarn

Three fine yarns including a rayon chenille, and two cottons for machine knitting (see Instructions for Using Coned Yarns on page 12) held together throughout. To substitute, use any combination of yarns held together, or one bulky-weight yarn to give the same gauge.

Yardage

850 (960, 1070) yards of each color.

Buttons

1/2"/1.25cm, 3.

Needles

Sizes 9 and 7, 16"/40.5cm circular needle in size 7.

Gauge

3 1/4 sts and five rows = 1"/2.5cm over St st using size 9 needles.

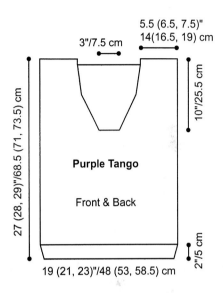

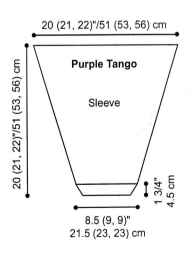

Instructions

Back

With smaller needles c.o. 62 (68, 74) sts. Work in 1 x 1 rib for 2"/5cm. Change to larger needles and work in St st. until piece meas 26 (27, 28)"/66 (68.5, 71)cm from beg.

Shape neck

Work 18 (21, 24) sts, join a second ball of yarn and b.o. center 26 sts, work to end. Working both sides at once, work even for 1"/2.5cm more, then b.o. each shoulder.

Front

Work same as back. When piece meas 17 (18, 19)"/43 (46, 48) cm shape neck: Work 25 (28, 31) sts, join a second ball of yarn and b.o. center 12 sts, work to end. Working both sides at once, b.o. one st at neck edge every fourth row 7 times until 18 (21, 24) sts remain at each shoulder. When piece meas the same as the back, b.o. all sts.

Sleeves

With smaller needles, c.o. 28 (30, 30) sts. Work in 1 x 1 rib for 1-3/4"/4.5cm. Change to larger needles and work in St st, inc one st each end of every row until 42 sts. Then, inc one st each end of every other row until 66 (68, 72) sts. When piece meas 20 (21, 22)"/51 (53, 56)cm, b.o. all sts.

Shawl Collar

Sew both shoulder seams. With circular needle, beg at lower edge of one side of neck opening, pick up 52 sts along side neck, 26 at back neck, and 52 along other side neck, but none along lower front edge–130 sts in all. Work in 1 x 1 rib for 4"/10cm, b.o. in ribbing. Overlap the two ends and sew to the sweater front.

Finishing

Sew on sleeves. Sew sleeve and side seams. Sew on the buttons placing them about 1"/2.5cm apart at the lower part of the collar. Make thread loops on the loose edge of the collar.

This blend of yarns including rayon chenille is a luxurious mix.

DESIGNING A CAP SLEEVE SWEATER

The shaped sleeve cap is not as difficult to design as it may appear; in fact, it is very easy to design a sleeve cap that will fit the sweater's armhole. A little extra planning will be needed to get the sweater to fit the way you want it to, so read through the instructions below, and for the two sweaters that follow—**Winter in Maine** and **Larkspur.**

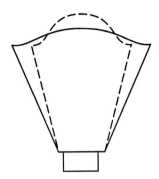

The shape of the sleeve cap is dependent upon the width of the upper sleeve (as demonstrated in the diagram here). A narrow upper sleeve results in a narrow, elongated cap. A wide upper sleeve makes a shorter and wider cap.

The cap of the sleeve is a different shape than the armhole. The armhole is indicated by the dashed line on the diagram accompanying the worksheet (page 75). The very uppermost part of the cap will fit the curve where arm meets shoulder, and the outer sections will be pulled into the curve of the shaped armhole of the sweater front and back pieces. The gaps (seen on the worksheet diagram between armhole and sleeve) show how bulk is reduced in the underarm area as compared to the straight sleeve sweater style.

Shaping the Armhole

The armholes of the front and back pieces of the sweater are indented anywhere from as little as 1" to as much as 3-1/2". Normally, one major decrease is followed by smaller ones to give the indent a rounded shape.

In planning the sweater, be aware of the measurement across the yoke area of the sweater. Stand with your arm at your side and observe the vertical line formed between your body and your arm. Continuing this line up to the shoulder gives the placement of the armhole seam. Measure across from one seam placement to the other, and you will have the width of the yoke. Multiply by the stitch gauge to find the number of stitches across the yoke, and make the armhole decreases accordingly.

Measurement x stitch gauge = number of stitches to knit for upper part of front and back pieces.

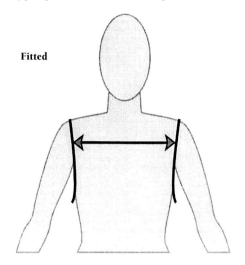

Fitted

Measure to find the width of the upper front and back pieces (yoke area) of the sweater. Sleeves can be fitted closely (above) or loosely (below).

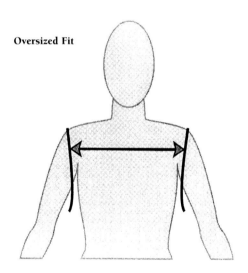

Oversized Fit

Shaping the sleeve cap:

1. You will need tape measure, paper, pencil, and scissors. The paper is for making a pattern; a sheet of newspaper will do, or tape sheets of paper together. First, knit the front and back pieces of the sweater.
2. Sew one shoulder seam and lay the sweater out flat.

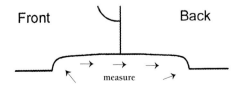

Front   Back

measure

Measure the entire armhole with the tape measure, then add about 1" extra, to make the sleeve cap just slightly larger than the armhole. A small amount of ease should be added to the cap, and when the cap is sewn to the armhole the ease is taken up into the seam.

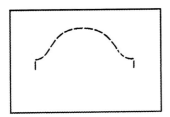

3. Using ⑥ of Measuring for Fit, indicate with the pencil on the paper the width of the upper sleeve. Take the tape measure and arrange it on its side to indicate the shape of a sleeve cap using the same length as determined in Step 2, above. Note how the cap follows a horizontal line at each end, and is rounded at the top. (This can also be done with a piece of string the same length as the measurement determined above. Arrange it as evenly as possible). Using a pencil, sketch along the string or tape measure.
4. Cut out the paper pattern then fold the pattern in half lengthwise to check that the sleeve cap is even from one side to the other. It's not likely to be, so take the scissors and trim it. Re-measure the cap. If you've

trimmed away too much, lay the pattern on another sheet of paper and sketch a new line that evenly adds the amount needed. Cut out the pattern.

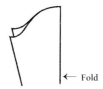

← Fold

5. Knit one sleeve up to the armhole, then shape the sleeve cap following the outline of the paper pattern. * Lay the knitting out flat on the pattern every few rows and bind off stitches as needed to follow the shape. Be sure to make bind offs evenly on both sides of the sleeve (a bind off made at the beginning of a RS row must be followed by an equal one made on the following WS row). B.o. the final sts. Write down the number and frequency of the bind offs, then follow your notes when knitting the second sleeve, OR graph the sleeve cap shaping, then make the second sleeve according to the graph.

When sewing the pieces of the sweater together, ease the sleeve cap into the armhole before sewing sleeve and side seams.

*Note: Since the length of the sleeve cap varies according to the width of the upper sleeve, it may be necessary to check that the length of the sleeve will be as intended. Sew both shoulder seams of sweater front and back, and put it on. Measure from the edge of the shoulder seam down to where the sleeve will end. Measure the sleeve up to the armhole, add the length of the cap and compare. Make any adjustments to the sleeve up to the armhole, then knit the cap.

CAP SLEEVE SWEATER WORKSHEET

Procedure:
   Do the worksheet Measuring for Fit (page 47)
   Choose a yarn and find gauges

stitch gauge = _____

row gauge = _____

① x stitch gauge = _____ stitches to knit for each of back and front.
Subtract 10 percent = _____ stitches for ribbing. . . . . ⟶

⑥ divided by 2 = _____ "(cm). . . . .
Subtract the result from ② = _____ "(cm).

② minus ④ (depth) = _____ "(cm): Begin neck bind-offs. .

④ (width) x stitch gauge = _____ total of stitches to bind off for neck.

⑤ x stitch gauge = _____ stitches for beginning of sleeve above ribbing. . . . .
Subtract 20 percent = _____ stitches for ribbing. ⟶

③ minus ① = _____ "(cm).
Divide the result by 2 = _____ "(cm): Length of sleeve to

▬ ▪ ▬ ▪ ▬ ▪ ▬ ▪ ▬ ▪ ▬ ▪ ▬

armhole.

⑥ x stitch gauge = _____ stitches at armhole.

⑤ x stitch gauge = _____ stitches above ribbing.

Subtract to =   _____ stitches to be increased. Divide by
                2 to = _____ total increase rows.

Subtract length of ribbing from sleeve length = _____ x row gauge = _____ total rows.

Divide by 2 = _____ RS rows.

Instructions

needle size for body of sweater _____

needle size for ribbing _____

Back

⟶ Cast on this number of stitches using the smaller needle size. Work desired length of ribbing. Change to larger needles, increase to the number of stitches to knit for the back.

⟶ Knit this length up to armhole. Work armhole decreases, then knit back to total length of sweater. Bind off all stitches.

Front

⟶ Knit the front same as for the back to here. Shape the neckline according to the instructions for your preferred neck style (pages 42 - 43). Work to same length as back and bind off all stitches.

Sleeves

⟶ Cast on this number of stitches using the smaller needle size. Work desired length of ribbing. Change to larger needles, increase to the number of stitches to knit for the sleeve.

Compare the increase rows with the total RS rows, and distribute increases evenly on RS rows to top of sleeve, or see Sleeve-increase Methods on page 41. Shape sleeve cap according to instructions on page 72. Make second sleeve the same. See page 43 for finishing the neck. Sew the pieces of the sweater together.

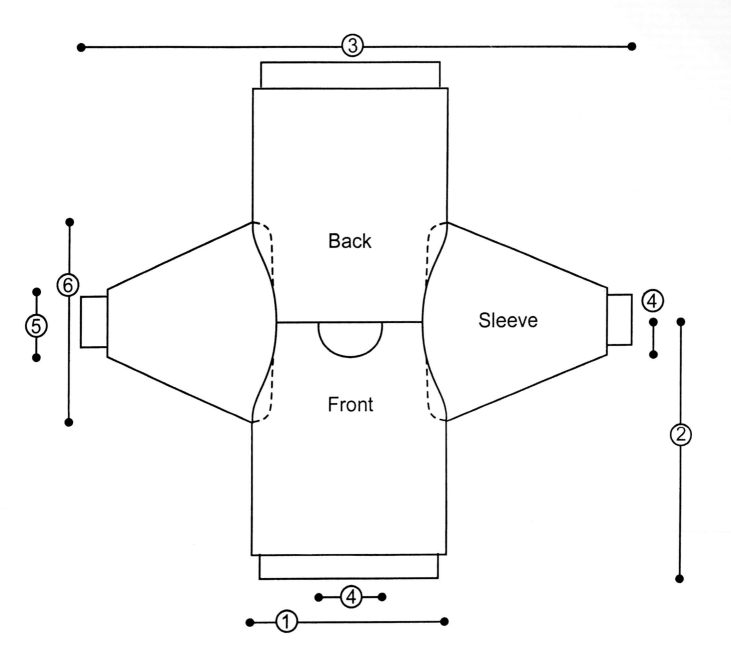

WINTER IN MAINE

One of my winter bundle-ups, I chose to make this sweater extra roomy (about 16" of ease in the circumference) with extra-long turtleneck and sleeve cuffs. The sleeve cuffs each have a thumb hole. The cap and upper sleeve are wide to have plenty of room to wear a shirt or two underneath. This one is good to wear while shoveling snow!

One way to repeat a color pattern is to mirror the design. Here, the design is mirrored from the bottom of the sweater to the upper area, with a slight variation used in the yoke. A touch of moss stitch occasionally used gives texture to the sweater. A stitch multiple of four is maintained throughout.

Sizes

Small (Medium, Large), with finished circumferences of 46 (50, 54)"/117 (127, 137)cm.

Yarn

Smooth, worsted weight wool in three colors: Cranberry, deep green, and taupe. Substitute with worsted weight wool yarns that obtain the same gauge.

Yardage

Approximately 1500 (1600, 1700) divided between three colors, with a little extra for the ribbing color.

Needles

Sizes 8 and 6.

Gauge

4-3/4 sts and 5-1/2 rows = 1"/2.5 cm over color and st pats using size 8 needles.

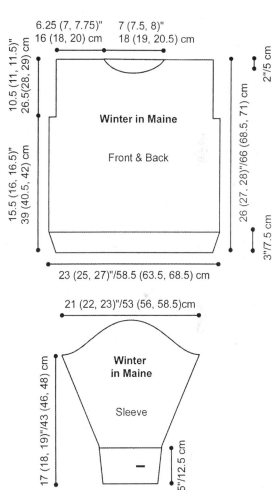

This cuff can be worn down over the hand, or folded up to the wrist.

Color and Stitch Key

◪ Dark Red

⊠ Dark Green

· Taupe

▣ P on RS, K on WS

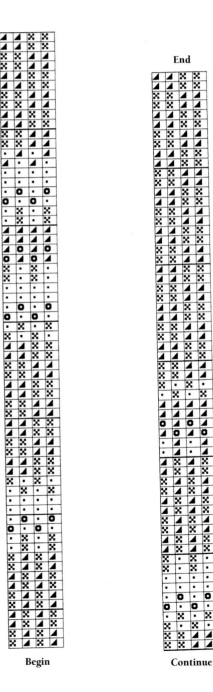

Begin   **Continue**   **End**

Instructions

Back

With smaller needles c.o. 98 (106, 114) sts. Work in 1 x 1 rib for 3"/7.5cm. Inc 12 (14, 14) sts evenly across last row—110 (120, 128) sts. Change to larger needles and begin color pat as charted, until 15-1/2 (16, 16 1/2)"/39 (40.5, 42)cm from beg. Shape armhole: (B.o. 4 sts at the beg of next two rows) twice, b.o. one st at the beg of next two rows–92 (102, 110) sts. Work in color pat without incs until piece meas 26 (27, 28)"/66 (68.5, 71) cm, then b.o. all sts.

Front

Work same as back. When piece meas 24 (25, 26)"/61 (63.5, 66)cm, shape neck: Work 33 (37, 41) sts, join a second ball of yarn, b.o. center 26 (28, 28) sts, work to end. Working both sides at once, dec one st at neck edge every row 3 (4, 4) times until 30 (33, 37) sts rem for each shoulder. When piece meas the same as the back, b.o. shoulder sts.

Right Sleeve

With smaller needles c.o. 36 (42, 46) sts. Work in 1 x 1 rib for 2 1/2"/6.5cm. To make thumb hole: On the RS, work 8 sts, b.o. the next four, work to end of row. Next row (WS), work up to bound off sts, c.o. four sts and work to end of row. Work even until cuff meas 5"/12.5cm. Inc 12 sts evenly across last row–48 (54, 58) sts. Change to larger needles and follow chart for color and stitch pats. At the same time inc one st each side of every RS row until 100 (104, 110) sts. Shape sleeve cap following the graph, following the shaping as given for all sizes (larger sizes will have a greater number of stitches to bind off at the top). Work second sleeve the same, but placing the thumb hole at the opposite side of the cuff.

Finishing

Sew one shoulder seam. Pick up 78 (82, 82) sts around neck and work in 1 x 1 rib for 8-1/2"/21.5cm, then b.o. in ribbing. Sew neck and remaining shoulder seam. Sew sleeve caps into armholes. Sew side and sleeve seams.

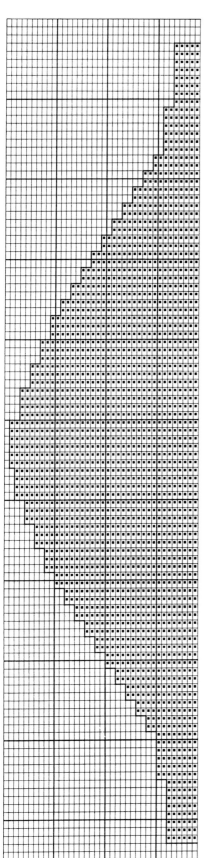

Sleeve cap for Winter in Maine

LARKSPUR

Pattern stitches show up sculpturally when they are worked in a plain wool yarn, especially when contrasted against the plain surface of the stockinette stitch. The cables, popcorn, and moss stitch panels making up the yoke of this sweater were designed by plotting on graph paper (see Combining Stitch Patterns on page 127). The pattern stitches make for a gauge of fewer stitches per inch than stockinette stitch, so, instead of adjusting the gauge of the pattern stitch yoke, it was used to "draw in" the yoke area, making the cap of the sleeve fit closer to the shoulder than it otherwise would have. The patterned yoke appears on both front and back of the sweater. The deep ribbings of the sweater bottom and sleeves are subtly increased by using three sizes of needles.

Size

Medium only, with a finished circumference of 44"/112cm. To make this sweater in a different size than that given, read through the instructions, then make your adaptations by using the worksheet *Cap Sleeve Sweater* (page 74).

To customize the size of this sweater design, first determine the width of the front/back pieces. Multiply by your stitch gauge, then fit this number of stitches to a ribbing multiple. The bottom ribbing used here is a multiple of 19 stitches. To adjust the width of the ribbing, change the number of ribbed stitches between the cables, thereby changing the multiple. Re-graph the pattern stitches for the yoke to fit the size needed.

Yarn

Smooth worsted weight wool, light blue heather. Substitute with worsted weight wool yarn that obtains the same gauge.

Yardage

1500.

Needles

Sizes 6, 7, and 8.

Gauge

4-1/4 sts and 5-1/2 rows = 1"/2.5cm over St st using size 8 needles.

Ribbing Stitch Pattern

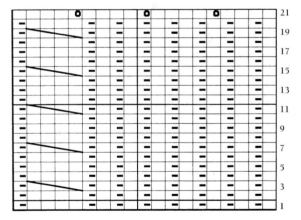

Cable and Bobble Stitch Pattern
rep 8 rows

Begin stitch patterns on row 5 →

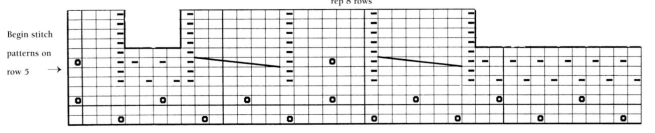

K on RS, P on WS | — P on RS, K on WS | O Bobble | C6B | C4B

Instructions

Back

With size 6 needles, c.o. 95 sts. Follow Ribbing st pattern. When ribbing meas 2"/5cm, change to size 7 needles. At 4"/10cm, change to size 8 needles. At 6"/15.5cm and on RS, knit across row making a PC every fifth stitch. P the following row. Work even in St st until piece measures 16"/40.5cm.

Armhole shaping

B.o. four sts at beg of next two rows, then one st at each end of every row three times–81 sts. Next RS row: Begin Cable and Bobble st pat according to graph. Work even in st pat until piece meas 27"/68.5cm, then b.o. all sts.

Front

Work same as back. When piece meas 24-1/2"/62cm, shape neck: Work 27 sts, join a second ball of yarn and b.o. center 27 sts, work to end. Working both sides at once, b.o. one st at each neck edge every other row three times, until 24 sts rem for each shoulder. When piece meas same as back, b.o. all sts.

Sleeves

With size 6 needles, c.o. 44 sts, work in K1 P1 ribbing for 2" (5 cm). Change to size 7 needles and inc one st at beg of row. Inc one st every 1"/2.5cm four more times at alternating ends of rows. At 4"/10cm, change to size 8 needles and work in pat to 6"/15.5cm–48 sts. On the next RS row change to St st and PC every sixth st. Inc one st each end of every RS row until 80 sts. Then inc one st each side of every other RS row until 94 sts. Work even until piece meas 18"/46cm. Follow the graph to knit the sleeve cap.

Finishing

Sew one shoulder seam. Using size 6 needles, pick up 72 sts around neck. Work in 1 x 1 rib for 7"/18cm. B.o. loosely in ribbing. Sew remaining shoulder and neck seam. Sew sleeve caps into armholes. Sew sleeve and side seams.

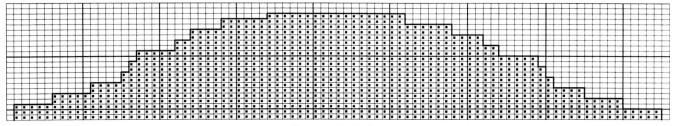

Sleeve cap for Larkspur.

DESIGNING A ONE-PIECE DOLMAN SWEATER

The dolman style is especially suitable for making short-sleeve, waist-length sweaters, while also lending itself to long-sleeve, longer sweaters. The one thing to keep in mind regarding the size of the sweater is that there are no shoulder seams to stabilize the shoulder area, so it could become stretched out of shape if the yarn is too heavy or the sleeves too large and heavy. And, because the fit of the sweater has more to do with drape than with seams following the lines of the body, consider yarns that will enhance the drape—lightweight wools, fine cottons, silks, and mohair are excellent possibilities.

The one-piece format of this style lends itself to many interesting treatments, such as those used in the following two sweaters. Both use mixed gauges, demonstrating how design areas can be incorporated into parts of a sweater. To knit a simple, basic dolman sweater, follow the *One-Piece Dolman Sweater* worksheet (page 84).

There are two ways to design a dolman sweater. One is to do all of the calculations and then knit according to the numbers. The other is to make a paper pattern using the basic dimensions, and then knit to follow the shape of the pattern. Do whichever is easiest for you after reading through the instructions below. Once you've made one, you will be able to refer to the sweater itself, and use it as a pattern for a next sweater.

To make a paper pattern, use newspaper or tape sheets together and, using pencil and a ruler or yardstick, make the pattern according to the dimensions derived from

Measuring for Fit (page 47) and the worksheet below.

When doing *Measuring for Fit*, ignore ⑥. For ①, use your body circumference at the bottom of the sweater adding a desired amount of ease.

Use the same number of stitches for the ribbing as for the beginning of the body of the sweater, especially for the front of the sweater. Increasing in this area (in addition to the side increases) can create an unwanted bulge.

When planning the increases along each side of the sweater, and to distribute them evenly, compare the number of RS rows with the stitches to be increased (see the worksheet). These two figures indicate how the increases will be spread over the distance. If the numbers come out equal (for instance 36 increase rows over 36 RS rows), simply increase one stitch at each end of every RS row. Or, if there are 36 increase rows and 72 RS rows, you will work increases on every other RS row.

If the numbers do not come out even, you can look for ways to make them even, such as by making the sweater body shorter or longer, or the widest part of the sweater narrower or wider. You can also work the increases unevenly by skipping an increase row here and there.

If the sleeves are long, there will be many stitches across the full width of the sweater. Use a long, circular needle. You will also need a short circular needle (16"/40.5 cm) to pick up and knit the neckline stitches afterwards.

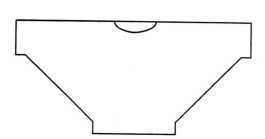
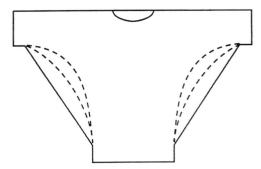

The diagram on the left shows the dolman shape given in the worksheet on the following page. That on the right shows how the length of the sweater and the shapes of the sleeves can be changed to create different styles.

ONE-PIECE DOLMAN SWEATER WORKSHEET

Procedure:
Do the worksheet Measuring for Fit (page 47)
Choose a yarn and find gauges

Stitch gauge = ____

Row gauge = ____

Note: To make it easier to calculate the main part of the sweater, body and sleeve ribbings are not included in the calculations below. Use the dimensions inside of the ribbing (keeping the ribbing in mind as part of the total dimensions).

① x stitch gauge = ____ stitches to begin front. ....

② minus 1/2 of ⑤ = ____ "(cm): Sweater length up to beginning of sleeve opening.

Multiply by row gauge = ____ number of rows along which increases will be distributed. Divide by 2 = ____ RS rows.

③ x stitch gauge = ____ stitches at widest part of sweater.

Stitches at ③ minus stitches at ① = ____ stitches to be increased.

Divide by 2 = ____ sts to be increased at each side of sweater. ....

② minus ④ (depth) = ____ "(cm)...................................

④ x stitch gauge = ____ bind offs for neck.

When sweater = ②: At back of neck CO the same number of stitches that were bound off (④ x stitch gauge).

⑤ x stitch gauge = ____ stitches for sleeve ribbing. ....

Instructions

Needle size for body of sweater ____

Needle size for ribbing ____

Front

Cast on this number of stitches using the smaller needle size. Work desired length of ribbing. Change to larger needles.

Knit up to the sleeve opening, distributing increases evenly (see page 41).

Work even up to neck shaping. Shape the neckline according to the instructions for your preferred neck style (pages 42 - 43).

Work even to end of sleeve opening, then begin decreasing to match the increases made for the front of the sweater.

Pick up and knit this number of stitches for the sleeve ribbings. See page 43 for finishing the neck. Sew up the side seams.

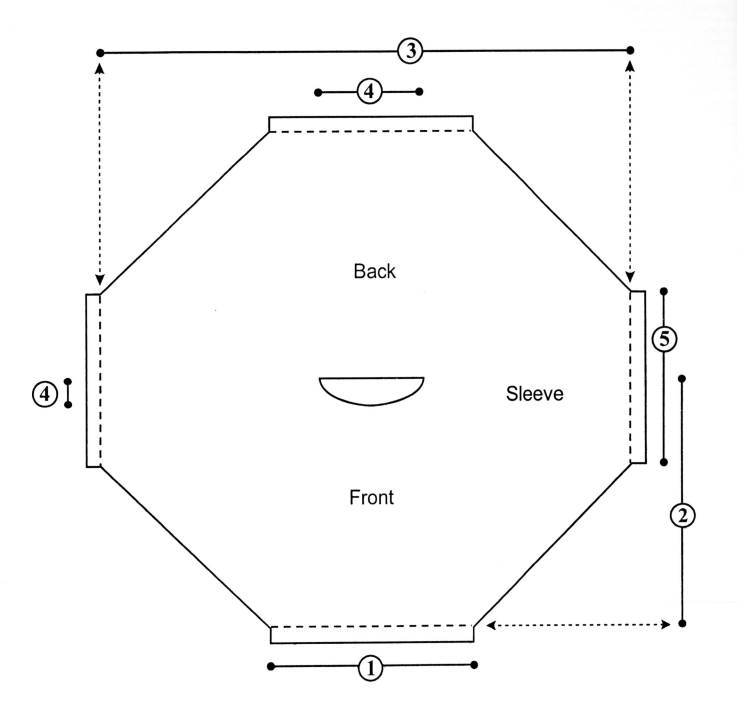

③

④

Back

Sleeve

④

⑤

Front

②

①

TEA PARTY

he lace panel in this sweater is a simple stitch pattern. The challenge of designing this
sweater was in combining stitch patterns that have two different gauges. To do a similar
design, make your calculations as best you can—and be prepared to fudge a little when
necessary!

The dolman style is readily adaptable to making small sweaters—waist-length and short-
sleeved—that are very comfortable to wear. This top fits to about 2"/5cm below the waist.
Although here made in wool, try the design in other fibers as well, such as cotton or linen for
summer wear, or rayon or silk for dressy occasions.

Size

Medium only, with a finished waistline circumference
of 30"/76cm, and length from shoulder of 20"/51cm. To
make other sizes, do *Measuring for Fit* (page 47) and the
worksheet *One-Piece Dolman Sweater* (page 84). Make the
length about 2" below waist, and the sleeve openings the
size of your choice. Draw the width of the lace panel onto
the worksheet diagram, then figure out how many stitches
to knit according to the gauges of the lace stitch and
stockinette stitch.

Yarn

A plain sport weight wool in purple. (Feel free to
substitute with any sport weight yarn that obtains the same
gauge.)

Yardage

860.

Needles

Sizes 6 and 4, 16"/40.5 cm circular needle size 4.

Gauge

4.4 sts and 6-1/2 rows = 1"/2.5 cm over St st, and 4 sts
= 1"/2.5cm over lace panel using size 6 needles.

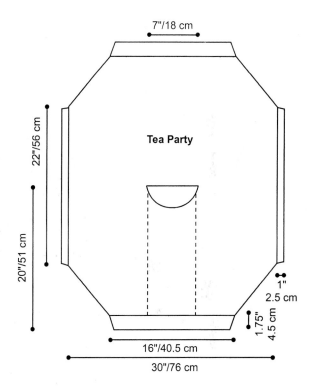

Lace Pattern

(mult of 2)
Row 1: YO, K2 tog.
Row 2: P.
Row 3: K.
Row 4: P. Rep these four rows for pat.

Instructions

Front

With smaller needles, c.o. 70 sts and work in 1 x 1 rib
for 1-3/4"/4.5cm, decreasing two sts within the last WS
row—68 sts. On the RS, change to larger needles and set up
the pat: 20 sts in St st, lace pattern over 28 sts, 20 sts in St
st. P next row. Continue in st pat and inc 1 st each end
every RS row—124 sts. Work even for 8"/20.5cm.

Neck shaping

Next row (RS): Work 50 sts, join a second ball of yarn,
b.o. center 24 sts, and work in pat to end. Working both
sides at once, dec 1 st at neck edge every row 5 times until
45 sts rem for each shoulder. Work even until piece meas
20"/51cm from beg.

 K on RS, P on WS   ☐ K 2tog   ⊞ Yarn Over

Back

C.o. 45 sts at back of neck–135, and work in St st for entire back of sweater. Work shaping as for front, but decreasing instead of increasing. End with 79 sts. Dec nine sts evenly spaced across next row–70 sts. Change to smaller needles and work in 1 x 1 rib for 1-3/4"/4.5cm. B.o. loosely in ribbing.

Finishing

With smaller needles, pick up 98 sts along each sleeve edge and work in 1 x 1 rib for 1"/2.5cm. With circular needles pick up 104 sts evenly around neck opening and work in 1 x 1 rib for 2"/5cm. Fold neck ribbing 1"/2.5cm to the inside and stitch in place loosely. Sew side seams.

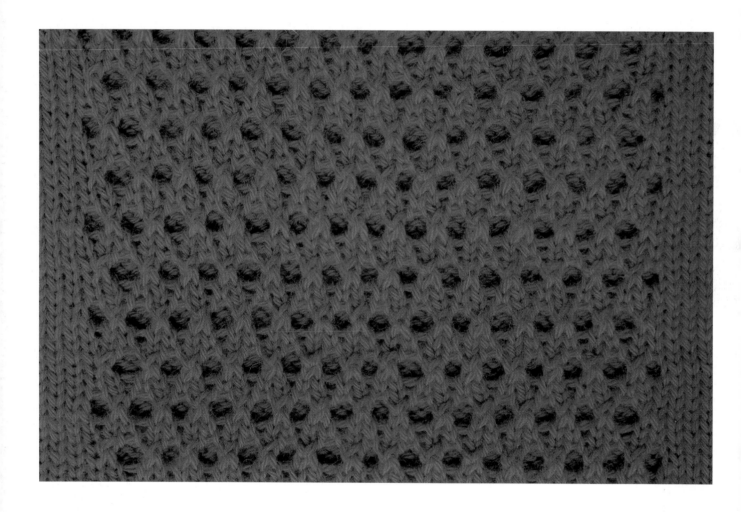

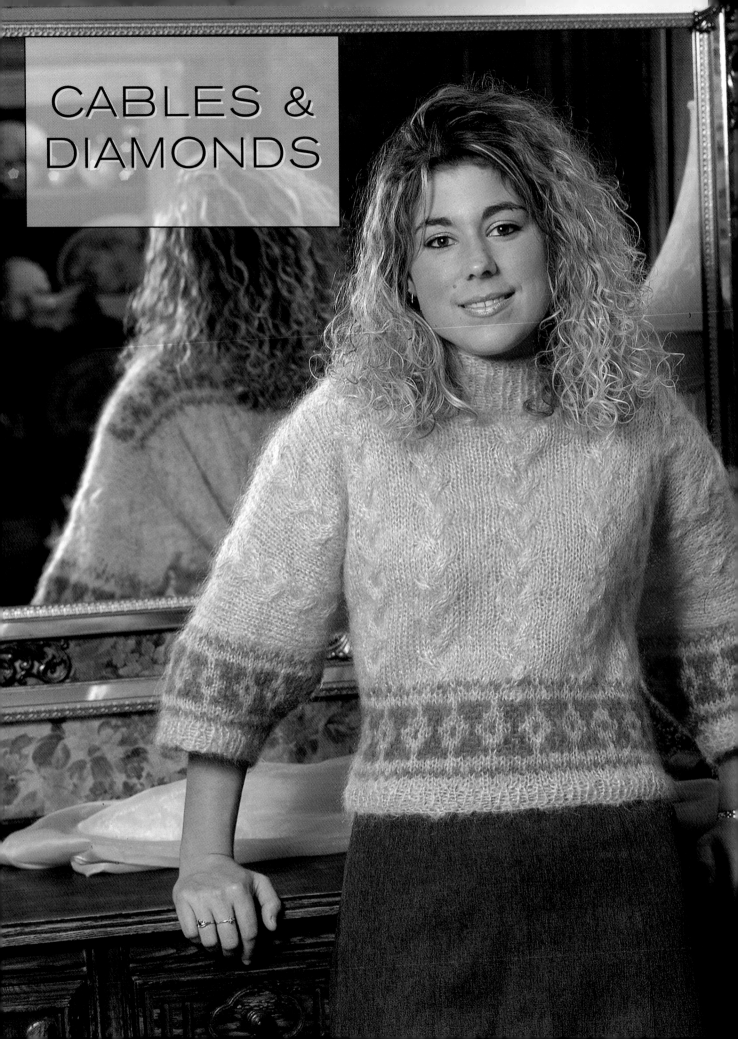

CABLES & DIAMONDS

Not for the faint-hearted, this was a challenging sweater to design for two reasons. First, two different gauges are used, and second, a color pattern is inserted within the stitch pattern in the shoulder area. The color pattern and the stitch pattern each have a different gauge and a different multiple.

Let a project such as this one challenge your knitting knowledge and instincts. The pattern is not written out for this sweater, because you will need to use your own dimensions for the sizing you require, fitting the different parts to it. The diagram of the sweater shown is given here, and you can form your own conclusions from it.

The front and back of the sweater are knitted in one piece that does not include the color pattern sections of the sleeves. Stitches are picked up along the sleeve edges and the color pattern is then worked, centering the design across the number of sts used.

There are several ways to accomplish a similar sweater:
1. Make very careful calculations, paying close attention to gauges and multiples.
2. Make a paper pattern, sketch in the different pattern areas, then knit to fit.
3. Make the sweater in separate pieces and sew them together at the end.

Begin by doing *Measuring for Fit* (page 47) and the worksheet *One-piece Dolman Sweater* (page 84), sketching the color pattern areas into the diagram. Decide how to tackle the project (see 1 through 3, above), and then proceed.

The yarn used here is a worsted weight mohair in pink (A) and rose (B). Needles in size 10 were used for the main parts of the sweater; size 8's were used for the ribbings. The gauges are 4 sts and 7 rows = 1"/2.5cm over the color pattern, and 5 sts and 5-1/2 rows = 1"/2.5cm over the cable pattern on the size 10 needles. The patterns and graphs for the cable and color patterns are given here.

Size

Medium only, with a finished waistline circumference of 32"/81.5cm, and length from shoulder of 20"/51cm.

Cable Pattern

(mult of 15)

The cable pattern consists of 9-st plaited cables on a background of St st

Rows 1: and 5: K

Row 2 and all WS rows: P

Row 3: K3, * C6F, K3, K6, * end with K3

Row 7: K3, * C6B, K6, * end with K3

Rep rows 1–8

Color Key

Dark Rose

Pink

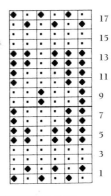

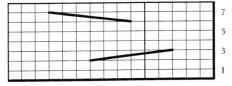

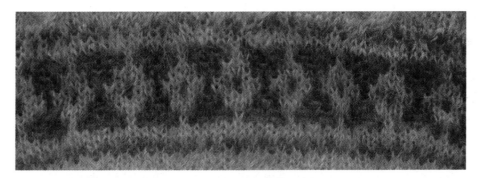

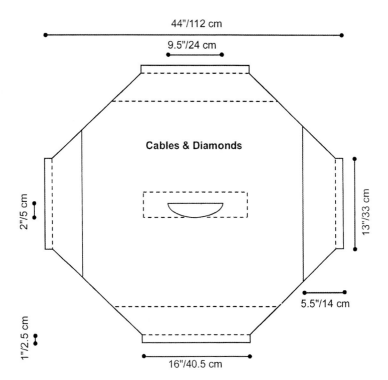

44"/112 cm

9.5"/24 cm

Cables & Diamonds

2"/5 cm

13"/33 cm

5.5"/14 cm

1"/2.5 cm

16"/40.5 cm

Designing a a Raglan Sleeve Sweater

Designing a raglan-sleeved sweater consists of making a sloping upper sleeve fit with the sloping armhole of the sweater body. It is easiest to do this by charting the pieces of the sweater on graph paper. The graph then becomes the pattern to follow as you knit. Refer to the diagram and graph for the **Woolly Bear** sweater on page 96 as an example as you plot your own graph.

Begin by selecting a yarn. Do a gauge swatch and determine needle size(s). Carefully measure for the gauges—both stitch and row gauges must be accurate for the success of the sweater. Do *Measuring for Fit* (page 47), then follow instructions below to graph the sweater pieces.

Use graph paper, or a computer cross-stitch or knitting program. If using graph paper, tape sheets together large enough for the rows (length) and stitches (width) of the back of the sweater. Other pieces, front and sleeves, can be plotted directly onto the graphed back of the sweater.

One square of the graph paper is equal to one stitch, and a row of squares is equal to one row of knitting.

Follow directions given on the worksheet *Raglan Sleeve Sweater* (page 94) to plot the individual parts of the sweater. Make an initial bind-off of 1/2"/1.25cm–1"/2.5cm to both upper sleeve and the beginning of the sweater armhole.

Two major determinants of the fit and style of the raglan sweater are the width of the upper sleeve and the depth of the armhole. The sleeve width is determined by ⑥. To find the depth of the armhole measure up from the bottom of the sweater to where you want the armhole to begin—the armhole can be quite low for an oversize

Different slopes fit together because the row count for each piece is the same.

sweater, or up near the armpit for a fitted sweater.

You can design a wide sleeve for a narrow sweater body, or a narrow sleeve for a wide sweater. In other words, the slope of the upper sleeve can be different from that of the sweater body. What is important is that the same number of rows be used for each, as they are sewn together row by row. In the swatches shown here, one slope was made by decreasing on every row, and the other by decreasing on every other row: different slopes, same number of rows, and they fit together perfectly.

Adding a color pattern to the sweater is as easy as adding the design onto the existing graph. Choose a design with a multiple that fits the body of the sweater, or adjust the number of stitches to fit the multiple.

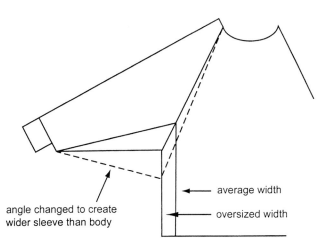

angle changed to create
wider sleeve than body

average width

oversized width

RAGLAN SLEEVE SWEATER WORKSHEET

Procedure:
  Do the worksheet Measuring for Fit (page 47)
  Choose a yarn and find gauges

Stitch gauge = _____

Row gauge = _____

① x stitch gauge = _____ stitches to knit for each of back and front. ....

② minus 1/2 of ④ (depth) = _____ "(cm) x row gauge = _____ rows. ....

④ (width) = _____ "(cm) x stitch gauge = _____ sts at top of sweater. ....
Measure up from the bottom of the sweater to the point where you want the armhole to begin = _____ "(cm) x row gauge = _____ rows. ....

⑥ x stitch gauge = _____ = stitches at widest part of sleeve.

⑤ x stitch gauge = _____ = stitches for beginning of sleeve above ribbing.

③ minus ④ = _____ "(cm) divided by 2 = _____ "(cm): Length of sleeve up to armhole x row gauge = _____ rows. Subtract, and begin graphing just above the ribbing.

To Knit the Sweater

Follow the graph adding ribbed cuffs: Use 10 percent fewer stitches for back and front ribbings, and 20 percent fewer for sleeve cuffs. Knit the four pieces, then sew sleeves to body leaving one seam unsewn. Pick up stitches around neckline and rib to the length desired. B.o. loosely. Sew all remaining seams.

You will need: graph paper (tape sheets together) or a cross-stitch or knitter's computer program.
  Note: ④ (depth) is the width of the top of the sleeve only, not to the bottom of the neck opening.
Needle size for body of sweater _____

Needle size for ribbing _____

Using the worksheet to graph a sweater

Back

→ Determine the width of the body of the sweater on the graph beginning above the ribbing.
→ Use the row gauge to indicate total length of sweater on the graph.
→ Center the stitches for the top of the sweater on the graph.
→ Graph the slope between beginning of armhole and top of sweater beginning with an initial bind off of about 1/2" to 1".

Front

Determine the shape of the front neck opening, and graph the neck opening onto the graph for the back.

Sleeve

Begin plotting the sleeve on the same graph.
  Center the stitches for ④ (depth) at top of graph.
  The length from armhole to top is the same number of rows as the front and back of the sweater.
  Plot the increases between sleeve bottom and armhole, and the slope of the upper sleeve using the same initial b.o. as for the sweater front and back.

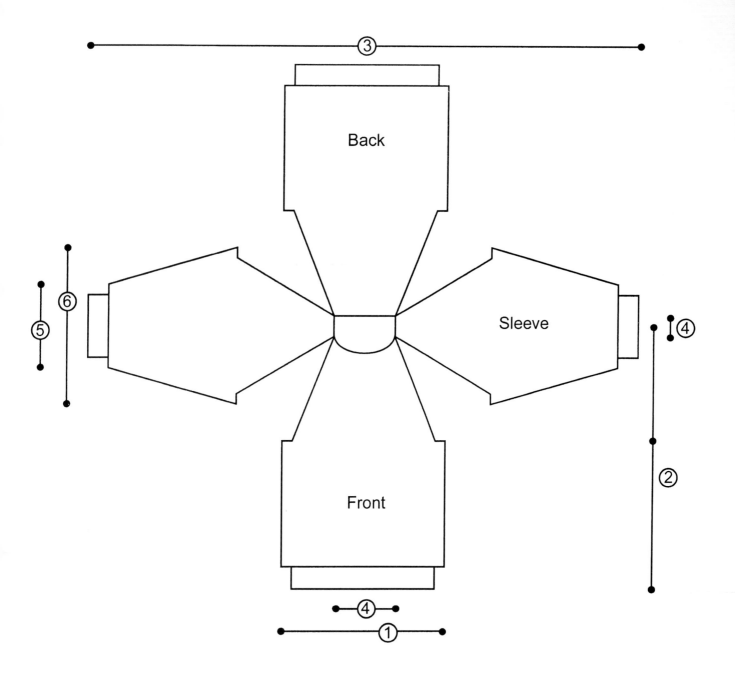

WOOLY
BEAR

This sweater apparently looks as cuddly as it feels, because when I wear it people seem to want to touch it! A variegated mohair yarn makes an interesting background for a subtle color pattern confined to the upper and lower parts of this sweater. The color pattern came about by doodling on graph paper.

Size

Medium only, with a finished circumference of 46"/117cm.

Yarn

Bulky weight mohair, brown variegated, and small amount of denim. Substitute with mohair yarns that obtain the same gauge.

Yardage

850 of main color (MC), small amount of second color (SC).

Needles

Sizes 10 and 8.

Gauge

3-1/2 sts and 4-1/2 rows = 1"/2.5cm over St st using size 10 needles.

Color pattern is a multiple of 6.

Use Raglan Shaping as given on page 41.

Work all selvedge sts, and RS decrease sts in MC.

Instructions

Back

With smaller needles and MC, c.o. 70 sts. Work in 1 x 1 rib for 1-3/4"/4cm ending on a WS row. Next row (RS): Change to larger needles and work in St st and SC, and inc 8 sts evenly spaced across row–78 sts. Begin color pat on following RS row according to chart. Complete color pat then work even until piece measures 13-1/2"/34cm, then follow graph working raglan shaping and color pat to top. B.o. all remaining sts.

Front

Work same as back until piece measures 24-1/4"/61.5cm. Shape neck: work up to b.o.'s on graph, b.o. center sts, fasten on a second ball of yarn for each color, then work to end of row. Working both sides at once,

follow the graph for shaping and color pat. B.o. remaining sts.

Sleeves

With smaller needles and MC c.o. 26 sts. Work in 1 x 1 rib for 2-1/2"/6.5cm ending with a WS row. Next row (RS), change to larger needles and St st and SC, increasing 2 sts evenly spaced–28 sts. Begin color pat on following RS row. Follow chart working color pattern and sleeve shaping to top of sleeve. B.o. remaining sts.

Finishing

Sew 3 of the 4 raglan seams. Using smaller needles, pick up 76 sts around neckline and work in 1 x 1 rib for 3". Bind off loosely. Sew remaining raglan seam and neck seam. Fold neck 1-1/2"/4cm to the inside and stitch loosely. Sew sleeve and side seams.

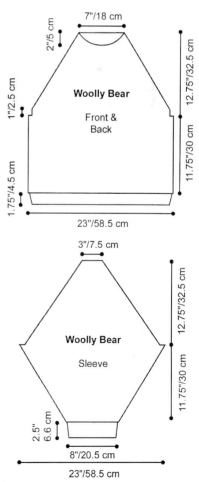

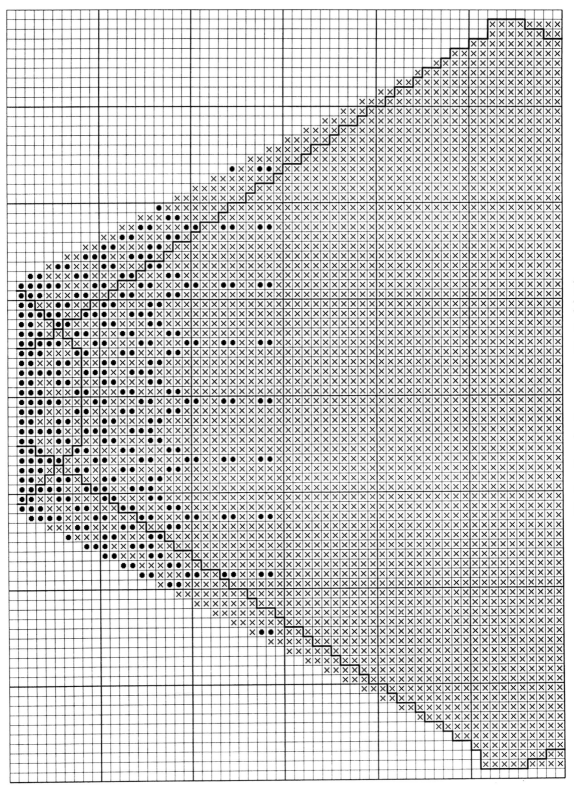

(Continuation of pattern on page 99; attach here)

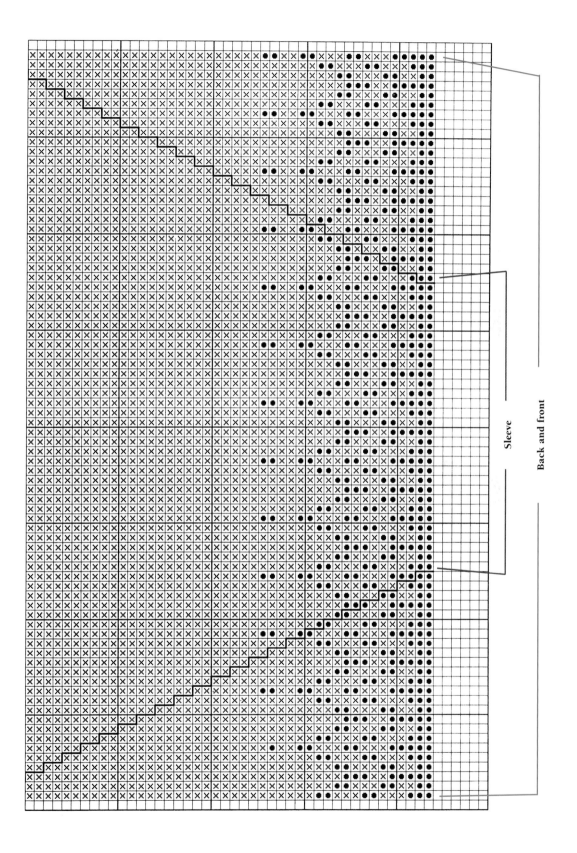

Sleeve

Back and front

DESIGNING FOR COLOR-WORKING

Fair Isle is a method of knitting with two or more colors in which yarns not in use are carried along the back of the work. Normally, only two colors are used in one row, and both hands are used to carry the yarns so the knitting can proceed quickly. It is easy to develop simple, geometric color patterns, either in the knitting, or on graph paper. This is a great way to use up leftover yarns. Yarns should be of similar gauges, but can be a mix of types. Experiment by making swatches using some of the color patterns given with the following sweaters. Then try devising some of your own.

Designing for Fair Isle Knitting

Begin with simple geometrics, such as squares, rectangles, and triangles. See the following sweaters for some examples. Designs can be created in the knitting, by doodling on graph paper, or by using a cross-stitch or knitter's computer program.

In each row, keep color areas to a maximum of five stitches per color to avoid long floats.

When planning a sweater, establish a multiple (see Multiples and Stitch Gauges on page 19).

Knit swatches of your ideas in various color combinations to see how the patterns look in different colors. See the following sweaters for some simple pattern ideas to begin with. Assemble several compatible colors and begin to knit a sweater!

Here are some Fair Isle techniques:

- The technique for handling the two yarns consists of holding the main color over the right-hand forefinger, and the secondary color over the left-hand forefinger (reverse for left-handedness). As you knit or purl along, use the appropriate color as needed. Picking up the left-hand yarn with the needle is kind of a "scooping" action, unlike the right forefinger, which wraps the yarn around the needle. Although this technique is a bit of an exercise to learn, once you do learn it, it is possible to knit quickly.

- The color not being knitted is carried along the back of the work and is called a "float." Keep the floats a bit loose—if pulled tight, they will cause the knitted piece to pucker. Keeping the stitches spread out on the needle just after they are knitted can prevent puckering. Knit a few stitches, spread them out, and repeat. (Or, on the other hand, *use* the puckering to create a unique sweater fabric!)

- If floats are long, they can be woven into the knitting. As you knit, hold the next stitch back (away from yourself), and bring the float in front of it, then knit the stitch over the float. Floats should not strand over more than five stitches, or they will make a loopy mess of the back of your knitting and will catch on things when you wear the sweater.

- Where colors are sharply contrasting, it is best to plan that lighter colors only are woven in. Woven-in floats have a tendency to show through.

TWO STEP

A sweater like this one is a good place to begin if you are new to two-color knitting. I've graphed the patterns, but suggest that you try your own creative color changing using two colors and looking for ways to vary the design. Try doing this "in the knitting," rather than on graph paper so you can watch the design develop in the colors.

In making this sweater, I worked out the color patterns while knitting, inventing as I went along. After establishing two sets of color pattern rows (see "Color Pattern 1" and "Color Pattern 2" on the graph), the goal became to see how many different ways they could be used.

Once the patterns are determined they may be mixed, matched, and repeated in various ways. One variation is implicit—substituting color A for color B in each of the color patterns. No matter what you do, you are likely to end up with a harmonious design for your sweater because the basic elements do not change.

Throughout the sweater, after two 2-color rows are worked, two plain rows follow. If you are a beginner to two-color knitting, you will find that using plain rows in a design has its advantages. Working them allows correcting of any mis-gauges that may have occurred in handling the two colors, and gives a brief respite in learning to work with two colors, which of course makes the sweater go faster.

Sizes

Small (Medium, Large), with finished circumferences of 36 (40, 44)".

Yarn

This sweater is made of two specialty yarns, both knitting ribbons. One is a cream-colored cotton/rayon blend, and the other is a blue, 100-percent rayon. Both are worsted weight. Substitute with any two worsted weight yarns that obtain the same gauge.

Yardage

988 (1097, 1208) divided between two colors.

Needles

Sizes 8 and 4.

Gauge

5 sts and 5-1/2 rows = 1"/2.5cm over color pattern and St st using size 8 needles.

Color pattern is a multiple of four.

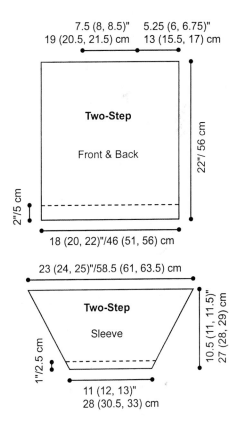

7.5 (8, 8.5)"   5.25 (6, 6.75)"
19 (20.5, 21.5) cm   13 (15.5, 17) cm

Two-Step

Front & Back

22"/ 56 cm

2"/5 cm

18 (20, 22)"/46 (51, 56) cm

23 (24, 25)"/58.5 (61, 63.5) cm

Two-Step

Sleeve

10.5 (11, 11.5)"
27 (28, 29) cm

1"/2.5 cm

11 (12, 13)"
28 (30.5, 33) cm

Instructions

Back

With smaller needles and the lighter color, c.o. 92 (100, 112) sts and work in St st for 2"/5cm ending with a WS row. Change to larger needles and work color pat following chart to top or until 22". B.o. all sts. Make the front same as the back.

Sleeves

With smaller needles and MC, c.o. 56 (60, 64) sts and work in St st for 1"/2.5cm ending with a WS row. Change to larger needles and work color pat following chart. At the same time inc one st each end every RS row until 116 (120, 124) sts. Work even in color pattern until the piece meas 10-1/2 (11, 11-1/2)"/26.5 (28, 29)cm, then b.o. all sts.

Finishing

Sew shoulders. To clean finish edge of neck opening, turn the edge to the inside approx 1/4"/.75cm at center and tapering to nothing at shoulders, stitch in place. Sew on sleeves. Sew sleeve and side seams. Turn 1"/2.5cm of lower edge of back and front to inside and stitch in place loosely. Turn 1/2"/1.25cm of lower edge of sleeves to inside and stitch.

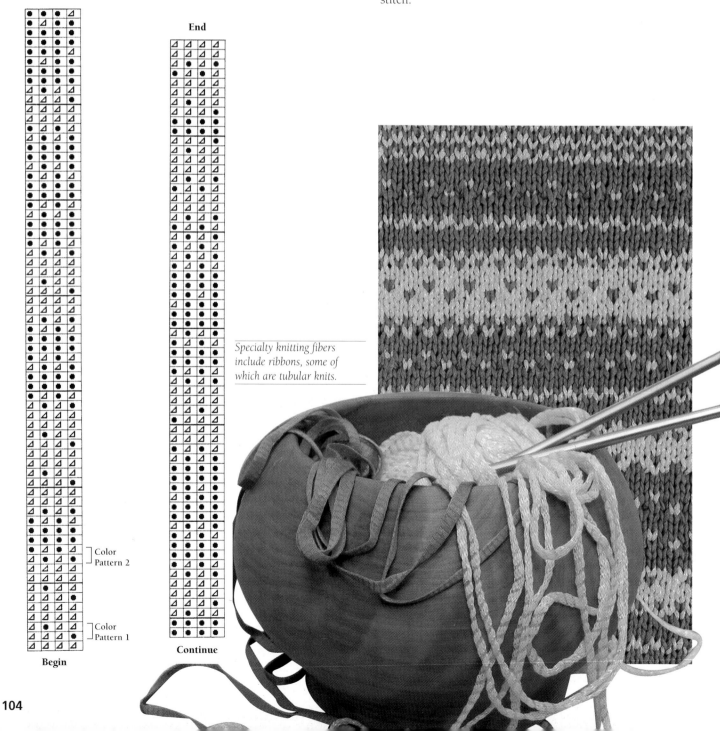

End

Begin

Continue

Color Pattern 2

Color Pattern 1

Specialty knitting fibers include ribbons, some of which are tubular knits.

SCRAP
BAG
MEDLEY

Designed in the knitting, my objective was to not repeat any of the color-working. I was happy to get to the top of the sweater because I found myself running out of ideas! This sweater is made of plain knitting wools plus a blue mohair. It is a scrap bag sweater (made of leftover yarns), and a favorite because it fits comfortably. I like how the design and the colors—teal, burgundy, blue, and taupe—came together.

The color pattern, too, is a "scrap bag" of multiples. As it was designed while knitting, I did not become concerned about how many different multiples surfaced. If the color pattern had been graphed first, the design would have been adjusted to fit one or two. Allow yourself a sense of artistic license in knitting a similar sweater. You can try re-graphing this color pattern, or try ad-libbing one of your own in the knitting.

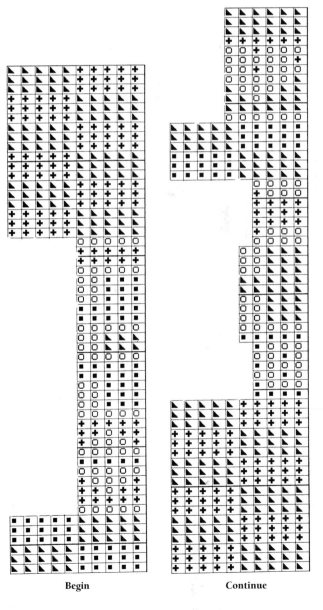

End

Begin   Continue

Yarn

Use any worsted weight wool yarns that obtain the same gauge (one can be mohair), four colors.

Tip:

Save your leftovers from knitting projects. Small bits of colors can be used in color-worked designs as accents with larger amounts making up the bulk of the colors. Select colors that work well with each other.

Size

Medium only, with a finished circumference of 45"/112cm.

Needles

Sizes 8 and 6.

Gauge

Four sts and five rows = 1"/2.5cm over color pattern and St st using size 8 needles.

Color Key

◤ Cranberry

✚ Blue

▢ Taupe

▪ Teal

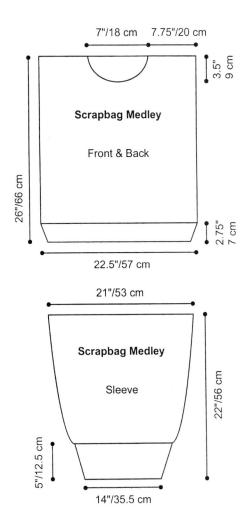

7"/18 cm   7.75"/20 cm

3.5"/9 cm

Scrapbag Medley

Front & Back

26"/66 cm

2.75"/7 cm

22.5"/57 cm

21"/53 cm

Scrapbag Medley

Sleeve

22"/56 cm

5"/12.5 cm

14"/35.5 cm

Instructions

Back

With smaller needles, c.o. 82 sts. Work in 1 x 1 rib for 2-3/4"/7cm. On the last row, inc eight sts evenly spaced across row–90 sts. Change to larger needles and begin color pat from chart on the next RS row. Work until the piece meas 26"/66cm, then b.o. all sts.

Front

Work same as back. When the piece meas 22-1/2"/57cm, shape neck: Work 34 sts, join a second ball of yarn for each color and b.o. center 22 sts, work to end. Working both sides at once, b.o. 1 st at neck edge every other row three times, until 31 sts remain for each shoulder. When the piece measures the same as for the back, b.o. shoulder sts.

Sleeves

With smaller needles, c.o. 38 sts. Work in 1 x 1 rib for 5"/12.5cm. On the last row, inc 18 sts evenly spaced across row–56 sts. Change to larger needles and begin color pat from chart on the next RS row. At the same time, inc one st each end every fourth row until 84 sts. Work even until the piece meas 22"/56cm, then b.o. all sts.

Finishing

Sew one shoulder. Using size 6 needles, pick up 72 sts evenly around neckline and work in 1 x 1 rib for 8-1/2"/21.5cm, then b.o. loosely in ribbing. Sew rem shoulder and neck seam. Sew on sleeves. Sew sleeve and side seams.

This color patterning is very similar to **Two-Step** (page 102), except that more colors are used. The patternings were designed in the knitting, and are based on a multiple of four. From the bottom of the sweater to the top, the design does not repeat, and note that the sleeves are not a repeat of the sweater body design. Because the "motif" is simple (1 and 1, 2 and 2, with an occasional plain row), and the colors blend with each other, the sweater as a whole appears neither "busy" nor incoherent.

The accompanying chart gives some, but not all, of the color patterns used. It is best if you make your own decisions regarding which patterns and colors to use. Then you will be able to knit a four-stitch color pattern without needing to carefully follow a chart. It's wonderful to watch a pattern grow as you knit, especially if that pattern is your own.

Yarn

A smooth, sport weight wool in five colors of your choice (taupe, denim, rose, burgundy, light blue are the colors used for the sweater shown) that obtains the same gauge.

Sizes

Small (Medium, Large), with finished circumferences of 34 (38, 42)"/86 (96.5, 106)cm.

Needles

Sizes 6 and 4.

Gauge

5-1/2 sts and rows = 1"/2.5cm over color pat and St st using size 6 needles.

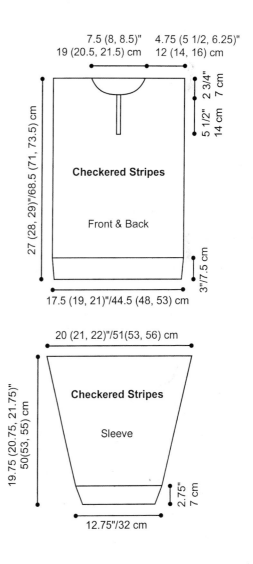

7.5 (8, 8.5)"
19 (20.5, 21.5) cm

4.75 (5 1/2, 6.25)"
12 (14, 16) cm

2 3/4" 7 cm

5 1/2" 14 cm

Checkered Stripes

Front & Back

27 (28, 29)"/68.5 (71, 73.5) cm

3"/7.5 cm

17.5 (19, 21)"/44.5 (48, 53) cm

20 (21, 22)"/51(53, 56) cm

Checkered Stripes

Sleeve

19.75 (20.75, 21.75)" 50(53, 55) cm

2.75" 7 cm

12.75"/32 cm

Color Key

☒	Taupe
◉	Cranberry
◢	Denim
▪	Lt. Blue
▢	Rose

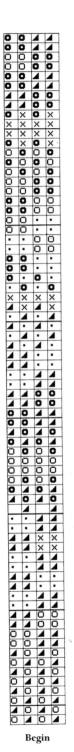

End

Continue

Begin

Back

With smaller needles c.o. 86 (94, 104) sts and work in 1 x 1 rib for 3"/7.5cm. Change to larger needles and St st, work one plain row, and inc 10 (10, 12) sts evenly spaced across row–96 (104, 116) sts. On the following row begin working the color pats from chart. Work even in pat until piece meas 27 (28, 29)"/68.5 (71, 73.5)cm, then b.o. all sts.

Front

Work same as back. When the piece measures 18-3/4 (19-3/4, 20-3/4)"/47.5 (50, 53)cm, beg front opening: Work 47 (51, 57) sts, join a second ball of yarn for each color and b.o. center two sts, work to end. Working both sides at once, work even until piece meas 24-1/4 (25-1/4, 26-1/4)"/61.5 (64, 67)cm, then shape neck: B.o. 16 (16, 18) sts at each neck edge, then one st each row five times until 26 (30, 34) sts remain for each shoulder. When the piece meas the same as the back, b.o. shoulder sts.

Sleeves

With smaller needles c.o. 40 sts and work 1 x 1 rib for 2-3/4"/7cm, then change to larger needles and increase 30 sts evenly spaced across the row–70 sts. On the next RS row begin color pat from chart. At the same time, inc one st each end of every fourth row until 110 (116, 122) sts. Work even until sleeve is 19-3/4 (20-3/4, 21-3/4)"/50 (53, 55)cm, then b.o. all sts.

Finishing

Sew both shoulders. Using smaller needles, pick up 100 (100, 104) sts around neck beg and ending at front opening. Work in 1 x 1 rib for 2-1/4"/6cm, then b.o. loosely in ribbing. To finish front opening, work three rows of single crochet around the entire opening, dec at bottom point so sts lie flat. *Or* pick up sts along entire opening, and work in 1 x 1 rib for 3/8"/1cm, dec at the bottom point so sts lie flat, then b.o. in ribbing. Sew on two metal clasps.

FIESTA

A wide-shaped neckline, short front opening which is more decorative than functional, and wide sleeves are the distinguishing details of this sweater—in addition to its bright, happy color patterning. A fancy silver pin somehow seems right for its closure.

The color patterning is repetitive from bottom to top of the sweater, but the colors change with each repeat, and the sleeves repeat a section of the sweater body design. As it was designed in the knitting—and I took my usual artistic license (see **Scrap Bag Medley** on page 106)—the pattern for the actual sweater is slightly different than that given in the chart. The charted one is a multiple of five throughout.

Yarn

Smooth sport weight wool in the colors of your choice (rust, fuchsia, purple, gray, and loden green are the colors used for the sweater shown) that obtain the same gauge.

Sizes

Small (Medium, Large), with finished circumferences of 42 (46, 50)".

Needles

Sizes 5 and 3.

Gauge

Six sts and seven rows = 1"/5cm over color pat and St st on size 5 needles.

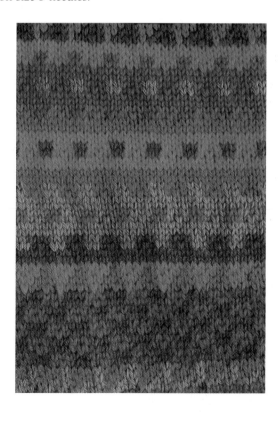

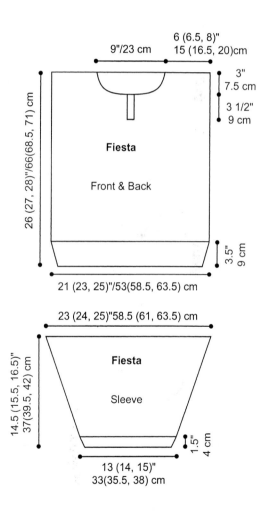

Color Key

◢ Moss

● Purple

☐ Fuschia

✖ Rust

▪ Grey

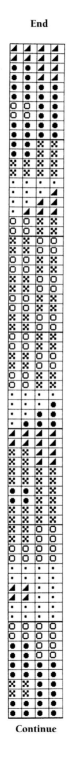

End

Continue

Begin

Instructions

Back

With smaller needles, c.o. 112 (120, 135) sts. Work in 1 x 1 rib for 3-1/2"/9cm. On the last row, inc 13 (15, 15) sts evenly spaced across row–125 (135, 150) sts. Change to larger needles and begin color pat from chart. Work even until the piece meas 26 (27, 28)"/66 (68.5, 71)cm, then b.o. all sts.

Front

Work same as back. When the piece meas 19-1/2 (20-1/2, 21-1/2)"/49.5 (52, 54.5)cm, beg front opening: Work 59 (64, 71) sts, join a second ball of yarn for each color, and b.o. 7 (7, 8) sts, work to end. Working both sides at once, work even until the piece meas 23 (24, 25)"/58.5 (61, 63.5)cm. At beg of next row inc 0 (0, 1) sts, and beg neck shaping: B.o. 6 sts at each side of neck opening every other row four times, until 35 (40, 48) sts rem for each shoulder. Work even until the piece measures same as back, then b.o. shoulder sts.

Sleeves

With smaller needles, c.o. 70 (76, 80) sts. Work in 1 x 1 rib for 1-1/2"/4cm. On the last row, inc 10 sts evenly spaced across row–78 (84, 90) sts. Change to larger needles and begin color pat from chart and at same time inc one st each end every other row for 3"/7.5cm, then every fourth row until 138 (144, 150) sts. When the piece meas 14-1/2 (15-1/2, 16-1/2)"/37 (39, 42)cm, b.o. all sts.

Finishing

With smaller needles, along one side of front opening pick up 21 sts and work in 1 x 1 rib for 1"/2.5cm, then b.o. in ribbing. Rep for other side of opening. Fold ribbing to inside and loosely stitch in place. Stitch bottom edges in place.

Neckband

Pick up 144 sts around neck opening including upper edges of opening ribs. Work in 1 x 1 rib for 1"/2.5cm, then b.o. loosely. Fold to back and hem in place. Sew on a metal clasp, or use a fancy pin to close the opening.

PLANNING A FRONT OPENING

It's sometimes nice to have a sweater that opens—if you are getting too warm, for instance, or to wear it partly open—or not "on" at all, but as a shoulder wrap.

A front opening can be added to any style of sweater.

A front opening can be centered or not, full-length or partial (placket). Decide where on the front you want it, then apportion the front sts accordingly.

The convention for a man's sweater is to put the buttonholes on the left, and for a woman's on the right—but this is *only* a tradition; I pay no attention to it and do most of my buttoned sweaters with the buttons on the "man's" side.

Button bands are commonly worked in K/P ribbing, but bands can also be made in garter, seed, or other stitches. Use needles two sizes smaller than those used for the main parts of the sweater to help ensure a firmer edge.

Here are three ways to add a band to a sweater:

- Knit the bands separately and sew them on. Cast on the number of stitches needed for the width of the band, and knit to the length required. The bands can be sewn on as they are being knitted (see **Autumn Tones** on page 122).
- Knit the bands onto the sweater by picking up and knitting along the sweater's edge. Use a long circular needle if necessary. Knit to the width of the band, then bind off loosely.
- Knit the band along with the fronts of the sweater. This method uses the same needle size as for the body of the sweater and will lack the firmness that it would have if knitted on a smaller needle size.

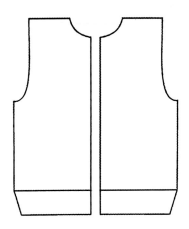

The calculations for the width of the button band in planning a sweater are as follows. You need to know the width of the sweater (① of *Measuring for Fit*).

Decide on the width of the button band.

① minus width of band = _____ "(cm) x stitch gauge for the sweater = _____ stitches.

Distribute the stitches evenly on either side of the opening.

Make the button band first. If it is made separately, sew it onto the sweater front. Sew the buttons onto the band. Then knit the buttonhole band, making the buttonholes to match the placements of the buttons.

Before beginning the buttonhole band, have the buttons handy. Make a swatch of the band and work a buttonhole in it to find the right size opening. Depending on the size of the button, bind off the center one, two or three stitches, and work to the end. On the next row cast on the same number of stitches above those bound off, and continue to knit the band.

Here are some ideas to consider if you wish to try using button bands creatively. To design bands such as these it may be easiest to either graph the sweater or make a paper pattern to follow as you knit. Since these bands may be purely decorative, make sure the neckline allows the sweater to be put on and off over the head. (The centered band is on the back of the sweater.)

RUSSIAN JACKET

The opening of this sweater was moved over to one side of the neck. The turtleneck can be worn open as a collar, or buttoned up. Sleeves knitted plainly in stockinette stitch contrast with the pattern stitch of the body of the sweater.

This is the first sweater I ever designed. It is made of a beautiful worsted weight wool yarn that began as a natural color, and was hand-dyed by my mother who, at the time, was beginning her exploration of spinning, dyeing, and weaving.

I had knitted a natural-colored wool sweater to be used as a store model at the yarn shop where I was employed. Like most sweaters that derived from commercial patterns of the time, the sleeves were way too tight, making the sweater uncomfortable and unwearable. The sweater nevertheless spent some time on display, after which I took it home, promptly ripped it out, and then sent the yarn to mom. When she sent it back, I was overjoyed to see the beautiful color it had become. Inspired to do something sensational with it, I soon abandoned my collection of knitting patterns, and began swatching to find a stitch pattern. With a vague idea in mind of making a side-buttoned sweater, the stitch pattern of choice soon made itself known, and the sweater came together with only a few rip-outs along the way. It has been one of my favorites ever since. Like a true classic, it never goes out of style.

With a stitch pattern like this one, the size of the sweater must be adapted to fit the repeats (instead of having the repeats adapt to a shape and size). Establish the number of repeats for the back. For the fronts, subtract one repeat for the button bands, and divide the remainder across the front.

Size

Medium only, with a finished circumference of 44-1/2"/113cm.

Yarn

A smooth worsted weight, high quality, resilient wool that obtains the same gauge.

Yardage

1800.

Buttons

9 buttons, 3/4"/2cm.

Needles

Sizes 8 and 6; cable needle.

Gauge

4-1/2 sts and 5-1/2 rows = 1"/2.5cm over St st, and 11 sts = 1-3/4"/4.5cm over 1 rep of pat st using size 8 needles.

Pat St.

(mult of 9 + 2)

Row 1: P2, K7, end with P2

Row 2 and all WS rows: K2, P7, end with K2

Row 3: P2, K1, (C2B) three times, end with P2

Row 5: P2, (C2B) three times, K1, end with P2

Rep Rows 2 – 5

The sweater back is 13 repeats of the pat, the right front is eight, the left front is four.

Instructions

Back

With smaller needles, c.o. 128 sts. Work in 1 x 1 rib for 2-1/2"/6.5cm, ending with a RS row. Next row (WS), change to larger needles, P, and inc 15 sts evenly spaced across row–143 sts. On next row begin the pat st and work even until the piece meas 20"/51 cm, then b.o. all sts.

Right Front

With smaller needles, c.o. 80 sts. Work same as Back, inc eight sts when changing to larger needles–88 sts. Work even until piece meas 8"/20.5cm. Shape neck: On a RS row (neck edge), b.o. 22 sts, then one st every row eight times until 44 sts rem for shoulder. Work even until the piece meas 20"/51cm, then b.o. all sts.

Left Front

With smaller needles, c.o. 40 sts. Work same as Back, increasing four sts when changing to larger needles–44 sts. Work even until the piece meas 20"/51cm, then b.o. all sts.

Sleeves

With smaller needles, c.o. 36 sts. Work in 1 x 1 rib for 2-1/2"/6.5cm, ending with a RS row. Next row (WS) change to larger needles, P, and inc four sts evenly spaced across row–40 sts. Working in St st, inc one st each end every third row until 98 sts. When the piece measures 19"/48cm, b.o. all sts

Turtleneck

Sew both shoulder seams. With smaller needles, pick up 92 sts evenly spaced around neckline including

1-1/2"/4cm along upper edge of left front. Work in 1 x 1 rib for 6-1/2"/16.5cm, then b.o. loosely in ribbing. Sew on sleeves, and sew sleeve and side seams.

Button Bands

With size 6 needles, c.o. eight sts and work in 1 x 1 rib for length of left front opening. Sew the band on. Sew on buttons beginning 3/4"/2cm from lower edge, the next one even with the top of the ribbed cuff, and the top button 3-1/2"/9cm down from the top, the next one 5-1/2"/14cm down, and the remainder evenly-spaced. Knit the second band, placing a buttonhole at each button placement. To knit the buttonhole, b.o. off the center two sts, and on the following row c.o. two at the center. Sew band to right front.

AUTUMN
TONES

Have you ever wanted a casual cardigan to toss on as you walk out the door? This easy-going style features a deep v-neck and fold-back sleeve cuffs. The narrow stripe in the ribbed cuffs is a decorative touch. Knitted in stockinette stitch with its colors used in wide stripes makes for a design that is easy to knit. It is a straight-sleeve style in which the sleeves are set into a slightly indented armhole.

This sweater was made of a palette of colors brought together by a common thread. Two different yarns are held together throughout, one is a sport weight in five shades, and the other a fingering weight in dark red. The finer, dark red yarn has the effect of deepening and enriching the colors of the sport weight yarns, while it blends the whole palette together. One of the blended colors was chosen for the sleeves of the sweater.

Try doing a similar sweater using colors of your own choice, blended throughout with one common color.

Sizes

Small (Medium, Large), with finished circumferences of 46 (50, 54)"/117 (127, 137)cm.

Yarn

One strand of wool sport weight yarn (in gray, purple, fuchsia, rust, and dark green) held together with one strand of wool fingering weight yarn in dark red. Substitute with five colors of a sport weight and a fingering weight wool yarn that together obtain the same gauge (the colors of your choice).

Yardage

1235 (1400, 1480) of dark red, plus same amount divided between five colors.

Buttons

1/2"/1.25cm wooden buttons, 6.

Needles

Sizes 7 and 5.

Gauge: 4-1/2 sts and 6-1/2 rows = 1"/2.5cm over St st on size 7 needles.

Color Pat for Ribbings

1 x 1 rib with four rows per color in the following sequence: gray, purple, fuchsia, rust, dark green.

Color Pat for Back and Front

10 rows per color following the same sequence as ribbing.

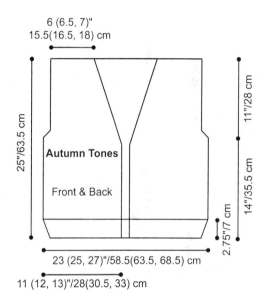

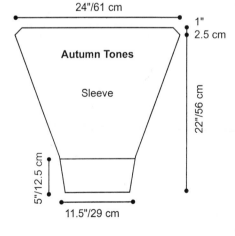

Note: At top of sweater back and fronts, end by knitting only five rows of the final color.

Five colors are each blended with a dark red, creating unity and harmony amongst the colors.

Instructions

Back

With smaller needles, c.o. 94 (100, 110) sts. Work in 1 x 1 rib following color pat for the ribbings, and inc 10 (12, 12) sts across the last row–104 (112, 122) sts. Next row (RS), change to larger needles, St st, and first color of color pat for back and front. Work even until the piece meas 14"/35.5cm.

Armhole Decreases

Dec one st each end of every row six times until 92 (100, 110) sts rem. Work even until piece measures 25"/63.5cm. B.o. all sts.

Fronts

With smaller needles, c.o. 46 (50, 54) sts. Work in 1 x 1 rib following color pat for the ribbings, and inc four sts across the last row 50 (54, 58) sts. Next row (RS), change to larger needles, St st, and first color of color pat for back and front. Work even until piece meas 13-1/2"/34cm. Beg neckline shaping: Dec one st at end of every fourth row. At the same time: When piece measures 14"/35.5 cm, beg armhole shaping: dec one st beg of every row six times. When 27 (29, 31) sts remain, work even until piece meas 25"/63.5cm. B.o. all sts. Work remaining front reversing the shapings.

Sleeves

With smaller needles, c.o. 46 sts. Work in 1 x 1 rib following color pat for the ribbings twice (making sleeve cuffs twice as long as for sweater body), and inc six sts across the last row–52 sts. Next row (RS), change to larger needles, St st, and sleeve color. Inc one st each end of every fourth row until 108 sts. Work even until piece meas 22"/56cm, then beg armhole shaping: Dec one st each end every row six times (12 sts decreased). When piece meas 23"/58.5cm, b.o. all sts.

Finishing

Sew shoulder seams. Sew on sleeves. Sew side seams.

Button band

With smaller needles, c.o. 8 sts. Work in 1 x 1 rib for about 10"/25.5cm. Leave sts on needle and begin sewing the ribbing to the sweater beginning at one lower front edge. For a woman's sweater, begin sewing to the left front. For a man's sweater, begin sewing to the right front. Continue to knit and sew, stretching the rib slightly at the back neck. Sew the buttons onto the band, placing the bottom button 3/4"/2cm up from lower edge, and the top button at beg of neckline shaping, and spacing remaining buttons between. Make buttonholes to match button placements while continuing to knit and sew on the ribbing. To make buttonholes, b.o. center two sts on one row, and c.o. two at the center of following row.

PICK UP AND KNIT

With this technique, you can add new knitting to an existing knitted piece. It is most often used for adding neckbands, turtlenecks, other neckline treatments, and button bands. Once you get to know it, you will find it marvelously flexible for other uses as well. Here are some ways this technique can come in handy:

- If you are unsure about how many stitches to use for the bottom and sleeve cuffs of a sweater, leave them for last. Before the sweater is sewn together, pick up and knit the ribbings. Then, if the cuffs are not right, they can easily be taken out and done over.

- Like the sweater, **Trompe L'Oeil**, following, it is easy to add sleeves to a short sleeved sweater. In the same way, you can add to the bottom of a sweater to achieve the look of a shorter sweater worn over a longer one. Pick up and knit to the length and shape desired.

- If you are making a straight sleeve sweater, the sleeves can be knitted directly onto the sweater. Knit the front and the back pieces, then sew both shoulder seams. (If you are working the neckband on two needles, sew one shoulder, pick up and knit the neckband, then sew the remaining shoulder.) Pick up the number of stitches needed for the upper sleeve, then knit from the top of the sleeve down to the cuff, reversing all shapings.

Other creative uses may also be found; for instance, try picking up and knitting stitches anywhere on a sweater for any special effects that you can imagine.

Directions for Picking Up Stitches

Measure the edge or area where stitches will be picked up, multiply by the stitch gauge, and pick up that number of stitches. If picking up to knit a ribbing, use the smaller needles as required for the sweater.

Note: Reverse the following directions if you are left-handed.

Working from right to left and using one knitting needle, insert the needle through the knitting, wrap the yarn around the needle and pull through. Repeat to pick up the number of stitches needed. Normally, the needle is inserted through two loops at the edge of the knitting.

When picking up for neckbands and other edgings, have the right side of the work facing you so you can easily see how and where to pick up a loop. The first row of knitting, then, will be a wrong side row.

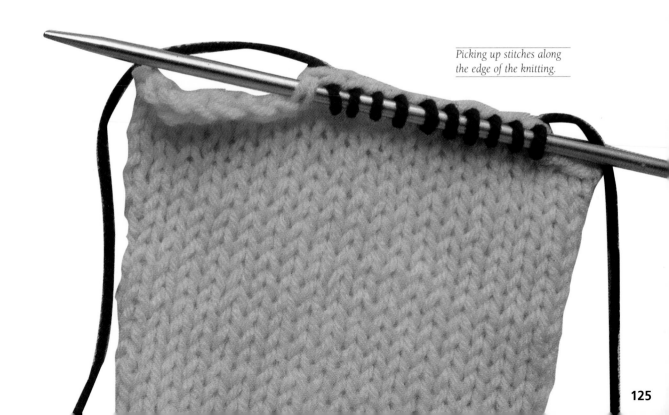

Picking up stitches along the edge of the knitting.

TROMPE L'OEIL

The technique of pick-up-and-knit is used here to create the look of one sweater worn over another when it is actually all one piece. This sweater is the same as **Tea Party** on page 86, with long sleeves added. My original idea was to create a sweater set consisting of a short-sleeved, lace-panel dolman top to be worn under a straight-sleeve cardigan. After knitting the one-piece top, I wondered if it would make sense to simply add sleeves to it, saving the knitting of the front and back pieces. So I picked up and knitted one sleeve, sewed the seams and tried it on. It worked out so well I did the second sleeve, and added a mock turtleneck to the sweater.

Working on the wrong side of the sweater, stitches were picked up along the base of the ribbing (where it attaches to the sweater). The side and sleeve seams of the sweater were first taken out so the piece could lie flat.

Yarn, needles, and gauge are the same as for Tea Party, page 86. You'll need approximately 450 yards of yarn.

Sleeve

Pick up 86 stitches on size 6 needles along the base of the sleeve ribbing. Work even for 3/4"/2cm, then dec one st each end every fourth row until 60 sts remain. At 14-3/4", change to size 4 needles and dec 14 sts evenly spaced across row–46 sts. Work in 1 x 1 rib for 2-3/4"/7cm, then b.o. loosely in ribbing. Rep for second sleeve. Sew sleeve and side seams.

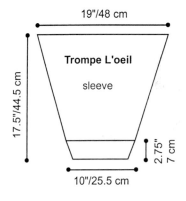

19"/48 cm

Trompe L'oeil

sleeve

17.5"/44.5 cm

2.75"/7 cm

10"/25.5 cm

Stitches for the sleeve are picked up at the base of the ribbing so the ribbing stays loose.

COMBINING STITCH PATTERNS

Magical worlds open up once you start working with either stitch patterns or color-working—or both. A kind of language begins to develop among the yarn, yourself, and the stitches. You learn the intricacies of the character of the yarn, and as your knowledge of stitch patterns grows, sometimes you can kind of sense what the yarn wants to do, and will do well. A broad horizon of possibilities opens up as you begin to realize that each combination of yarn, stitch pattern, and sweater shape can be unique and different.

Take your yarn of choice through its paces by trying different patterns in it. Stitch patterns, if chosen well, bring out the best qualities of the yarn. Every yarn shows off patterns differently. Experimenting like this is the only way to find combinations that speak to each other, to the yarn, and to you. Make swatches! The ones you don't use can be taken out and the yarn reused.

First, do *Measuring for Fit* (page 47) and choose a sweater style.

After you have swatched and found several stitch patterns to combine, begin to fit the patterns together. Do this by sketching the shape of the sweater, indicating the placements of the patterns on the sketch. Then determine the width of each of the patterns, adding or subtracting stitches to fit the size of the sweater. You may need to find a separate gauge for each stitch pattern; then work with the gauges to fit the width of the sweater.

It is often easiest to graph the patterns as they will be used on the sweater, adding any neckline and sleeve shaping to the graph. Then, the graph can be used as your pattern for the sweater. If your stitch patterns are intricate, it will be much easier to follow the design if it is graphed.

POLAR BEAR

Because of this sweater, I no longer own a coat. This sweater, with a windbreaker over it, is all I need on the coldest winter days outdoors. Bulky wool yarns make a thick, warm sweater, and a bulky wool sweater is not for the indoors (unless your heating system fails). If you have trouble staying warm in winter, this is the type of sweater to have—wool is an excellent insulator.

Smooth, bulky wool yarns are wonderful for showing off stitch patterns—especially since the stitches are much larger than in finer yarns. A simple cable has a dramatic effect.

Sizes

Small (Medium, Large), with finished circumferences of 44 (48, 52)"/112 (122, 132)cm.

Yarn

A bulky-weight wool with low twist that obtains the same gauge.

Yardage

1100 (1200, 1300).

Buttons

8 metal buttons, 7/8"/2cm, 1 metal clasp.

Needles

Sizes 10-1/2 and 9.

Gauge

Three sts and four rows = 1"/2.5cm over St st and Moss sts, cable panel = 5-3/4"/14.5cm wide using size 10-1/2 needles.

Moss Stitch

Row 1: (multiple of 2) * K1, P1 *

Row 2: * P1, K1 *

Rep these two rows

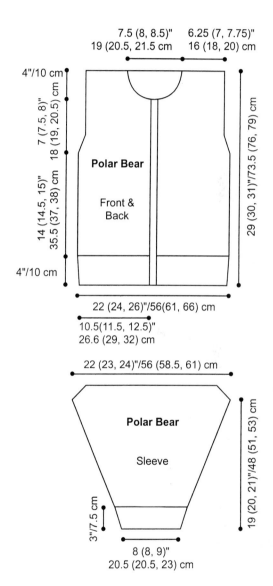

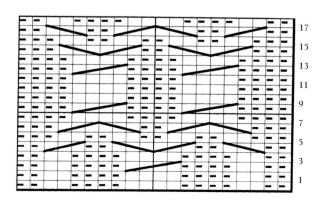

Cable Panel (see graph, left)

(worked on 22 sts)

Row 1: K1, P2, K2, P4, K4, P4, K2, P2, K1

Row 2 and all WS rows: Purl the knit, and knit the purl sts of previous row

Rows 3 and 19: K1, P2, K2, P4, C4B, P4, K2, P2, K1

Row 5: K1, P2, T3F, P2, T3B, T3F, P2, T3B, P2, K1

Row 7: K1, P3, T3F, T3B, P2, T3F, T3B, P3, K1

K on RS, P on WS	— P on RS, K on WS	 T3F	C4F	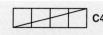 T3B

Rows 9 and 13: K1, P4, C4B, P4, C4B, P4, K1

Row 11: K1, P4, K4, P4, K4, P4, K1

Row 15: K1, P3, T3B, T3F, P2, T3B, T3F, P3, K1

Row 17: K1, P2, T3B, P2, T3F, T3B, P2, T3F, P2, K1.

Rep rows 1–20

Instructions

Back

With smaller needles, c.o. 72 (76, 80) sts. Work in 1 x 1 rib for 4"/10cm, ending with a WS row. Next row (RS), change to larger needles and set up pats as follows: Moss Stitch over 6 (6, 8) sts, Cable Panel over 22 sts, Moss Stitch over 16 (20, 20) sts, Cable Panel over 22 sts, and Moss Stitch over 6 (6, 8) sts. Work even in pats until piece meas 18 (18-1/2, 19)"/46 (47, 48)cm.

Shape Armhole

Dec one st every other row each side four times–68 sts. Work even until piece meas 29 (30, 31)"/73.5 (76, 79)cm, then b.o. all sts.

Left Front

With smaller needles, c.o. 34 (36, 38) sts. Work in 1 x 1 rib for 4"/10 cm, ending with a WS row. Next row (RS): Change to larger needles and set up pats as follows: Moss Stitch over 6 (6, 8) sts, Cable Panel over 22 sts, Moss Stitch over 6 (6, 8) sts. Work even in pats until piece measures 18 (18-1/2, 19)"/46 (47, 48)cm.

Shape Armhole

Dec one st beg of every RS row four times. Work even in pats until piece measures 24"/61cm.

Shape Neck

At the beg of the next WS row, b.o. 5 (5, 7) sts, then dec one st at the beg of each WS row three times. Work even in pats until piece meas 29 (30, 31)"/73.5(76, 79)cm, then b.o. all sts.

Right Front

Make the same as left front, reversing all shapings.

Sleeves

With smaller needles, c.o. 24 (24, 27) sts. Work in 1 x 1 rib for 3"/7.5cm. Change to larger needles and inc each side of every other row until 66 (70, 72) sts. Work even until piece meas 19 (20, 21)"/48 (51, 53)cm.

Shape Armhole

Dec each side of every other row four times–58 (62, 64) sts, then b.o. all stitches.

Button Band

With smaller needles, c.o. six sts. Work in 1 x 1 rib for length of front opening, then b.o. all sts. For a woman's sweater, sew button band to left front of sweater (right front for a man's sweater). Sew on eight buttons, having bottom button 1-1/2"/4cm from bottom of band, and top button 1"/2.5cm from top of band. Space others equally apart.

Buttonhole Band

With smaller needles c.o. six sts. Work in 1 x 1 rib, making a buttonhole at each button placement. To make buttonhole: B.o. center two sts, work to end. On the next row c.o. two sts at center. Sew band to sweater.

Neck

Sew both shoulders. With smaller needles, pick up 60 (60, 64) sts evenly spaced around neck. Work in 1 x 1 rib for 4"/10cm, then b.o. loosely. Fold neck 2"/5cm to the inside and sew loosely. Sew sleeves into armholes. Sew sleeve and side seams. Sew metal clasp to neck of sweater.

Sweaters entered the fashion world but are still practical garments.

DESIGNING A SWEATER IN SECTIONS

Separately knitted, vertical sections can be sewn together to form a sweater. This is an easy way to combine stitch patterns. Simply knit the widths needed to fit within the size limitations of the sweater design.

It is also a good way to use up leftover yarns. Make swatches of yarns of different colors and textures, then sew them together to see how they work together.

Although it is not essential that all gauges be the same, the yarns used should be *similar* in gauge. This is so the sweater fabric will be somewhat coherent.

Unite the scheme by choosing one yarn for all of the ribbings or edgings. Although any of the sweater styles can be used, the straight-sleeve style is easiest because less shaping is needed.

Instructions for Combining Sections

1. After doing Measuring for Fit, sketch a diagram of the sweater shape. The sweater can be made in one large piece as Cozy Cables (page 132). Or, you can make separate front and back pieces.

2. Pick a strategy for making sure all the parts will fit together. A full-size paper pattern is one way. Using newspaper, make a pattern the size indicated by your diagram. Another way is to measure, and keep measuring as you make the pieces. Either way, you will need to lay the pieces out on a flat surface as they are knitted to see how they will go together.

3. Make swatches of the pattern stitches you want to use, and plan the widths of the different sections of the sweater to fit together within the diagram or pattern.

4. Knit the pieces to make up the front and back of the sweater. When knitting the front sections, remember to do the neck shaping. (See Neckline Styles on pages 42 - 43.)

5. When the front and back pieces are completed, sew the pieces together at the shoulders and try it on to check the fit. Make any necessary adjustments.

6. Knit the sleeves by combining sections as for the sweater body, or use a plain stitch such as stockinette, knitting each as one piece. Sew on the sleeves.

7. Pick up and knit where ribbings are needed: bottom, sleeves, front openings, and neckline, making the ribbings the length desired. Sew any remaining seams.

Work up swatches of different patterns to find several that will work together.

COZY CABLES

This is my winter computing sweater, designed for sitting at the computer when I'm not active enough to stay warm. There are thumb holes in the extra-long sleeve cuffs so I can type (almost like gloves without the fingers). The turtleneck is also made extra long so when it is unrolled it covers up to my eyes keeping my nose warm. The sweater is long, and is buttoned so it can be opened in stages as I slowly warm up on a chilly day.

This is a "creative project," so specific instructions are not given except for the diagram. Follow instructions for designing a sweater in sections, adapting the design to your own needs and ideas.

The sweater shown here consists of four cable panels and five bobble insertions. The sleeves are in plain stockinette stitch. Ribbings are made a little more snugly than usual, are extra long, and contain thumb holes in the sleeve cuffs (for thumb hole instructions, see **Winter in Maine** on page 76). Two worsted weight yarns are used, a heather wool for the cable panels, and a navy wool for the bobble insertions and ribbings. Thirteen 3/4" buttons were needed.

Bobble Insertion.

(CO 5 sts.)

Row 1: P2, B, P2

Row 2: K

Row 3: P

Row 4: K

Rep these 4 rows for pat

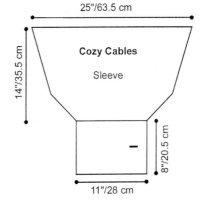

Cable Panel (see below)

CO 44 sts.

Row 1: K2, P2, C2B, P1, K4, P1, C2B, P2, K12, P2, C2B, P1, K4, P1, C2B, P2, K2

Row 2 and all WS rows: P the K, and K the P sts of prev row

Row 3: K2, P2, C2B, P1, C4F, P1, C2B, P2, C6F, C6B, P2, C2B, P1, C4F, P1, C2B, P2, K2

Rep these four rows for pat

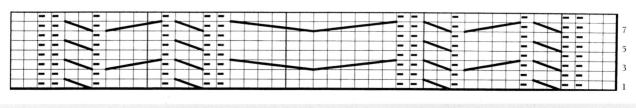

K on RS, P on WS   — P on RS, K on WS   O Bobble   C2B   C4F   C6F   C6B

DESIGNS FOR VESTS AND TOPS

A vest in its simplest form is a sweater without sleeves. Like a sweater, a vest can be made to fit closely or loosely. The cap-sleeve sweater style is the one to use to make a fitted vest because of the shaped armhole. Use the straight-sleeve sweater style to make an extended shoulder vest or a short-sleeve top. The dolman style is ideal for short-sleeve summer tops.

The armhole of a vest should be generous enough for a shirt to be worn underneath, but that of a top should be more closely fitted. Allow for any edge finish that will be added to the armhole—a ribbing or other edge stitch will extend the shoulder line and "shrink" the size of the armhole opening. Make these adjustments when doing the *Measuring for Fit* worksheet (page 47).

To Knit a Vest or Top

Knit the back and front pieces. Sew one shoulder. Pick up stitches along the neckline to knit the neck edging in ribbing or the stitch of your choice. Sew the remaining shoulder seam and neck edging. Pick up stitches along one armhole and knit the edging. Repeat for the second armhole. Sew the side seams.

As you would for a sweater, make the following decisions:

- Choose a neckline style:
  Boat neck
  Rounded
  Square
  V-shaped;

- Use any armhole shaping from:
  None
  To deeply-shaped;

- Have a front opening:
  Or not;

- Finish edges with:
  Ribbing, stockinette stitch (curled),
  Garter or other non-curling stitch,
  Hems;

- Make the vest:
  Long (tunic),
  Short (waist or shorter)
  Or in-between;

- Use a yarn that is:
  Fancy and textured, plain
  Or your creation;

- Choose from:
  A pattern stitch,
  Color-working,
  Or plain stitch.

BOUCLE
VEST

A vest in a plain style—in this case an oversized pullover with scooped neckline—makes a quick and easy project. It is knitted of a stylish, loopy mohair yarn (also called "boucle"), so textured it would be nearly impossible to follow the stitches if anything other than a plain stitch pattern were used. The reverse stockinette stitch was chosen because it has the effect of enhancing the loopiness of the yarn, with stockinette stitch to make the curled edgings.

Sizes

Small (Medium, Large), with finished circumferences of 38 (42, 46)"/96.5 (106, 117)cm.

Yarn

Loopy mohair (boucle) yarn in a worsted gauge.

Yardage

550 (650, 750).

Needles

Sizes 8 and 5.

Gauge

Four sts = 1"/2.5cm over St st using size 8 needles.

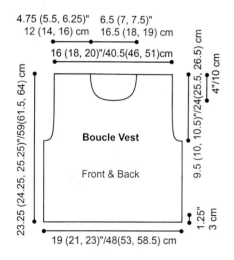

4.75 (5.5, 6.25)" 6.5 (7, 7.5)"
12 (14, 16) cm   16.5 (18, 19) cm

16 (18, 20)"/40.5(46, 51)cm

9.5 (10, 10.5)"/24(25.5, 26.5) cm

4"/10 cm

23.25 (24.25, 25.25)"/59(61.5, 64) cm

Boucle Vest

Front & Back

1.25"
3 cm

19 (21, 23)"/48(53, 58.5) cm

Back

With smaller needles, loosely c.o. 68 (76, 82) sts. Work in St st for 1-1/4"/3cm. Change to larger needles, begin RS and inc 8 (8, 10) sts evenly spaced across row–76 (84, 92) sts. Work even until piece meas 12-1/2 (13, 13-1/2)"/32 (33, 34)cm, then work armhole bind offs: B.o. four sts at the beg of next two rows, then one st each side every other row–64 (72, 80) sts remain. Work even until piece meas 23-1/4 (24-1/4, 25-1/4)"/59 (61.5, 64)cm, then and b.o. all sts.

Front

Work same as back until piece meas 19-1/4 (20-1/4, 21-1/4)"/49(51.5, 54)cm. Shape neck: Work 29 (33, 37) sts, join a second ball of yarn and b.o. center 18 sts, work to end. Working both sides at once, b.o. one st at neck edge every other row until 19 (22, 25) sts remain for each shoulder. When piece meas same as back, b.o. shoulder sts.

Finishing

Sew one shoulder seam. With smaller needles, pick up 74 (80, 84) sts around neck: 26 (32, 36) along the back neck, 15 along each side, and 18 along the front. Work 1-1/2"/4cm in St st, then b.o. loosely. Sew remaining shoulder seam. With smaller needles pick up 76 (80, 84) sts along one armhole. Work in St st for 1-1/4"/3cm, then b.o. Rep for other armhole. Sew side seams.

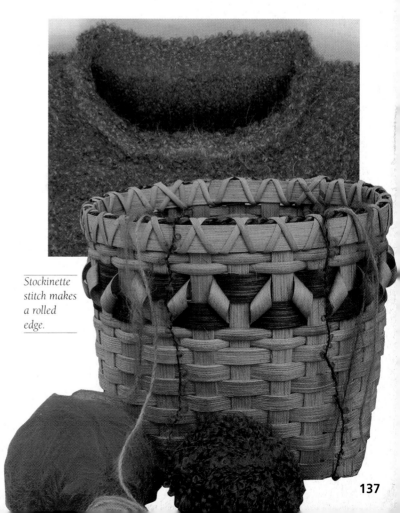

Stockinette stitch makes a rolled edge.

APPENDIX

MEASURING FOR FIT WORKSHEET

Fill out the information on this form for each sweater you design. Widths, lengths, and ease may vary for different styles. For more information on fitting a sweater, see pages 45 - 49.

The circled numbers correspond to those used on the worksheets for the individual sweater types.

Chest/bust measurement = _____ "(cm)

Amount of ease_____ "(cm)

Total_____ "(cm)

Total divided by 2 = _____ "(cm) ①

Shoulder to bottom of sweater = _____ "(cm) ②
Sleeve end to sleeve end = _____ "(cm) ③
Width of neck opening = _____ "(cm) ④
Depth of neck opening = _____ "(cm) ④
Lower sleeve circumference = _____ "(cm) ⑤
Upper sleeve circumference = _____ "(cm) ⑥

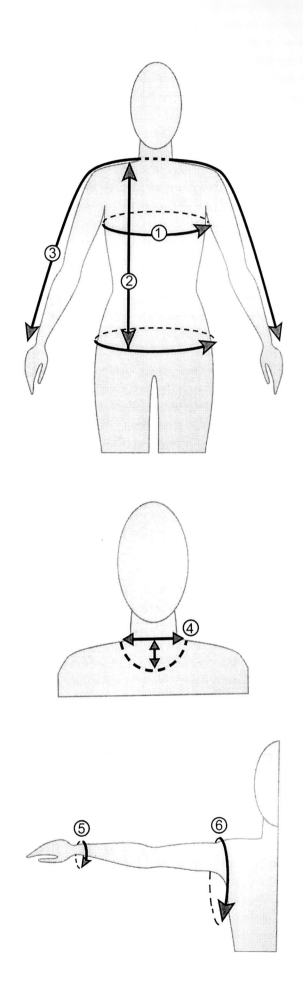

FINISHING A SWEATER

Careful finishing works wonders in obtaining a professional-looking garment. First, use a dull needle to darn in the yarn ends. Weave the ends horizontally through the backs of the stitches. Cut the ends leaving a short end so it doesn't work its way through to the front. If the sweater pieces require blocking, see page 15. Sew the remaining seams, matching any stitch and color patterns. First, align the seams to be joined and tie them loosely with a loop of yarn at intervals. Thread a blunt needle with the same yarn as the sweater—unless the yarn is a specialty type that will not sew easily. In that case, use a same-colored smooth wool yarn.

When sewing up the ribbings, join the edges of the stitches. When sewing up stockinette stitch areas, use the following technique.

Working just in from the edge stitch and working vertically, pick up two loops of two rows and pull through. Do the same on the other piece and continue. This makes an invisible joining.

To join a sleeve top to an armhole, work in a similar fashion, picking up two loops of two rows on one piece, and two loops of one row on the other.

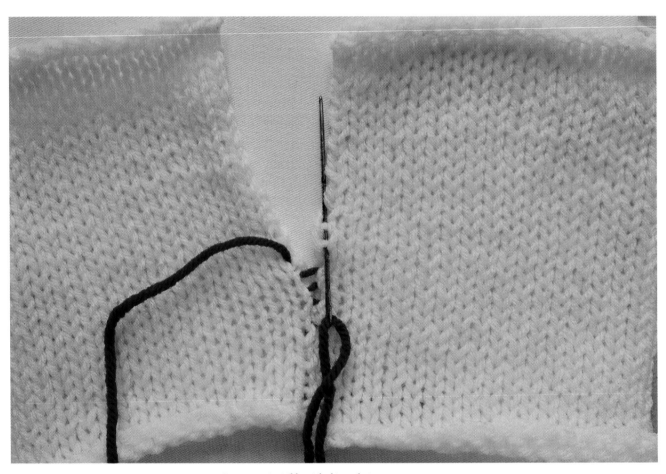

Seams are invisible with this technique.

KNITTER'S GRAPH PAPER
Photocopy as needed.

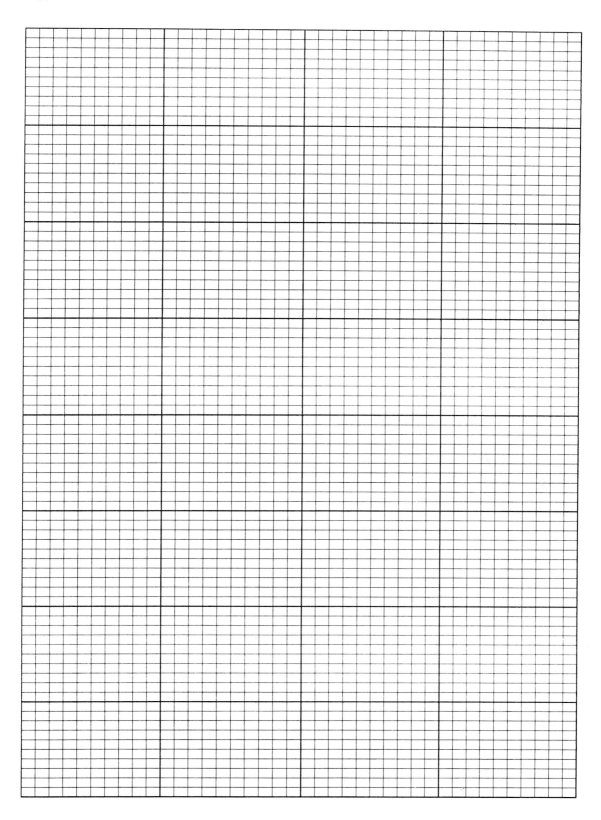

BASIC SWEATER DIMENSIONS

The table below is a compilation that is "averaged" from hundreds of sweater patterns published in book, magazine, and pamphlet form. Variations exist on all of the dimensions given. They represent a generic fit and do not include the ease required for wide sleeves, enlarged neck openings, or variations in body length.

You can knit a straight sleeve sweater directly from the chart. For other sleeve styles and variations, refer to the text.

The table gives a "standard fit" with an ease of 2".
To knit a fitted sweater: knit one size smaller.
To knit a loose-fitting sweater: knit 2 - 3 sizes larger.
To knit an oversized sweater: knit 4 - 6 sizes larger than the chest/bust size below.

Women's sizes are given in the unshaded columns, and men's in the shaded columns.

Other Standard Dimensions
Lengths to knit ribbings:
Bottom of sweater: About 2-1/2" for women's, and 3" for men's.
Sleeve cuffs: About 2-1/2".
Crewneck: Rib for 2", turn 1" to inside, and hem.
Mock turtleneck: 4" or longer.
Turtleneck: 6" or longer.

Depth of neckline: 2" – 3".

Size:	34 "/86 cm		36"/91.5 cm		38"/96.5 cm		40"/101.5 cm		42 "/106.5 cm		44"/112 cm		46"/117 cm		48"/122		To Knit a straight-sleeve sweater
Front/back width (circumference)	18" (36") 46 cm (91.5 cm)	18" (36") 46 cm (91.5 cm)	19" (38") 48 cm (96.5 cm)	19" (38") 48 cm (96.5 cm)	20" (40") 51 cm (101.5 cm)	20" (40") 51 cm (101.5 cm)	21" (42") 53 cm (106.5 cm)	21" (42") 53 cm (106.5 cm)	22" (44") 56 cm 112cm	22" (44") 56 cm 112cm	23" (46") 58.5 cm 117cm	23" (46") 58.5 cm 117cm	24" (48") 61 cm 122cm	24" (48") 61 cm 122cm	25" (50") 63.5cm 127cm	25" (50") 63.5cm 127cm	Multiply x stitch gauge for # of stitches to knit. Calculate ribbing.
Sweater length	20" 51 cm	24.5" 62 cm	21" 53 cm	25.5" 65 cm	22" 56 cm	26" 66 cm	22.5" 57 cm	26.5" 67 cm	23" 58.5cm	27" 68.5cm	25" 63.5cm	27" 68.5cm	25" 63.5cm	28" 71 cm	25" 63.5cm	29" 73.5cm	Knit back to this length. Front: do neck shaping as desired.
Sleeve end to sleeve end	54" 137 cm	54" 137 cm	55" 139 cm	56" 142 cm	56" 142 cm	57" 145 cm	57" 145 cm	61" 155 cm	58" 147cm	62" 157.5cm	60" 152cm	62" 157.5cm	61" 155cm	66.75" 169.5cm	64" 162.5cm	68" 173cm	Use to calculate sleeve lengths.
Total width of neckline opening	6.5" 16.5 cm	6.5" 16.5 cm	6.5" 16.5 cm	7" 18 cm	6.75" 17 cm	7" 18 cm	7" 18 cm	7.5" 19 cm	7" 18 cm	8" 20 cm	7.5" 19 cm	8.5" 21.5cm	7.75" 20 cm	8.5" 21.5cm	8" 20 cm	8.75" 22 cm	Multiply by stitch gauge for total stitches for neck bind-offs.
Lower sleeve circumference	7.5" 19 cm	7.5" 19 cm	8" 20 cm	8" 20 cm	8.5" 21.5 cm	8.5" 21.5 cm	9" 23 cm	9.5" 24 cm	9" 23 cm	10" 25.5cm	9" 23 cm	10" 25.5cm	9.25" 23.5cm	11" 28 cm	9.5" 24 cm	11.5" 29 cm	Multiply by stitch gauge to begin sleeve. Calculate ribbing.
Upper sleeve width	15" 38 cm	18" 46 cm	16" 40.5 cm	19" 48 cm	18" 46 cm	19" 48 cm	19" 48 cm	20" 51 cm	20" 51 cm	20.75" 53 cm"	21" 53 cm	21" 53 cm	21" 53 cm	22.25" 56.5cm	21.5" 55 cm	23" 58.5cm	Increase sleeve to this width.

INDEX

P

Q

R

S

T

V

W

Y